This belongs to

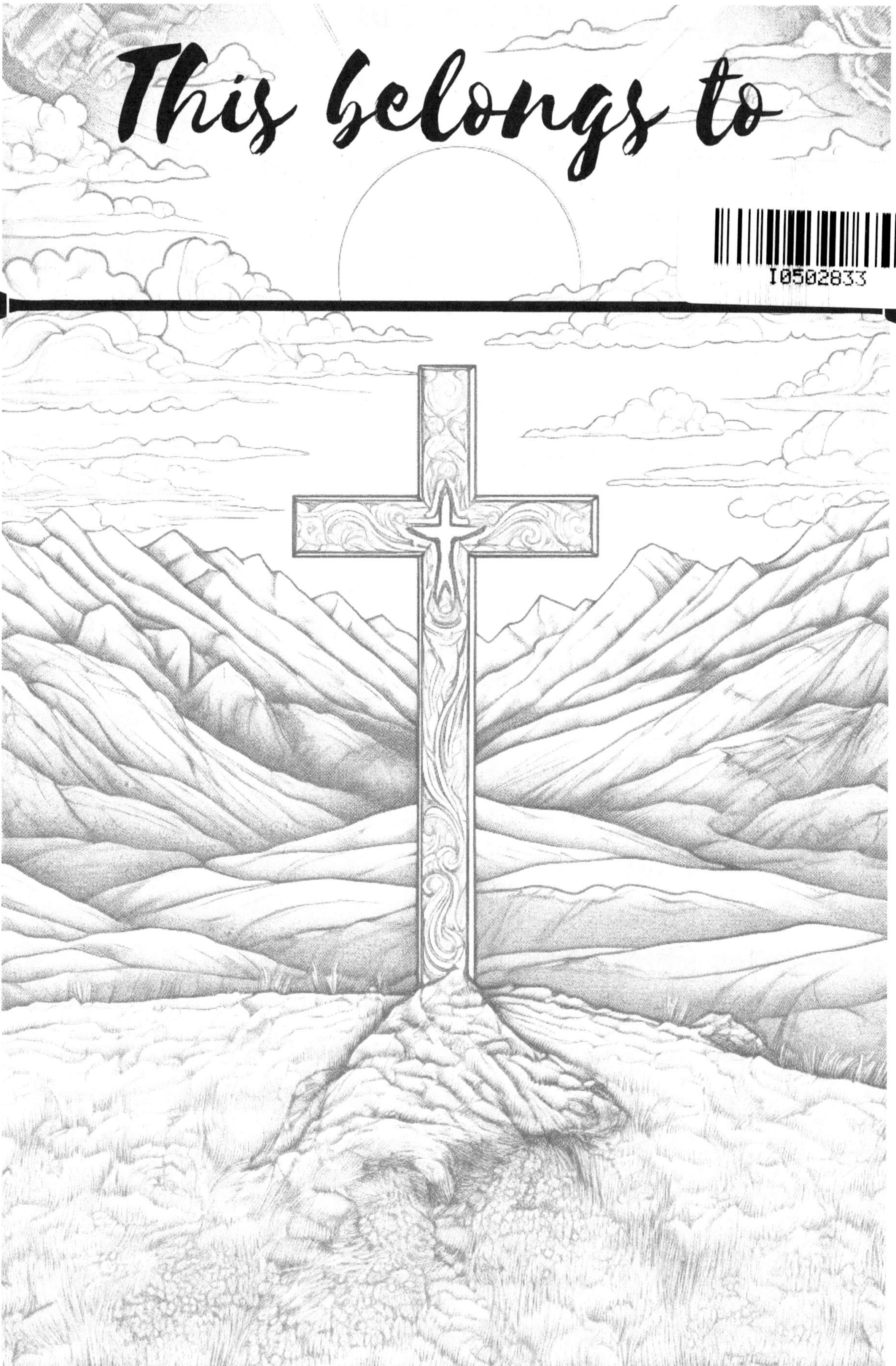

Contents

Page 1 - Contents

Page 2 - Summary

Page 3 & 4 - Matthew

Page 5 & 6 - Mark

Page 7 & 8 - Luke

Page 9 & 10 - John

Page 11 & 12 - Acts

Page 13 & 14 - Romans

Page 15 & 16 - 1 Corinthians

Page 17 & 18 - 2 Corinthians

Page 19 & 20 - Galatians

Page 21 & 22 - Ephesians

Page 23 & 24 - Philippians

Page 25 & 26 - Colossians

Page 27 & 28 - Thessalonians

Page 29 & 30 - 1 & 2 Timothy

Page 31 & 32 - Titus

Page 33 & 34 - Philemon

Page 35 & 36 - Hebrews

Page 37 & 38 - James

Page 39 & 40 - 1 Peter

Page 41 & 42 - 2 Peter

Page 43 & 44 - 1 John

Page 45 & 46 - 2 John

Page 47 & 48 - 3 John

Page 49 & 50 - Jude

Page 51 & 52 - Revelation

SUMMARY

The New Testament is a collection of 27 books in the Bible that tells the story of the life, teachings, death, and resurrection of Jesus Christ, as well as the early Christian church. It serves as a guidebook for believers, offering wisdom, guidance, and lessons for living a life of faith and following the teachings of Jesus. Through the New Testament, we learn about the importance of love, forgiveness, compassion, and the transformative power of faith. It also emphasizes the concepts of salvation, grace, and redemption, highlighting the central message of God's love and the offer of eternal life through Jesus. The New Testament invites us to explore the teachings and example of Jesus, providing valuable insights and inspiring us to grow spiritually and live according to God's principles.

Sermon on the Mount, which is a collection of teachings and sayings of Jesus found in Matthew chapters 5-7. In this sermon, Jesus presents a new interpretation of the Jewish Law and offers radical teachings on love, forgiveness, and righteousness that challenge the conventional wisdom of his time. The Sermon on the Mount is considered a cornerstone of Christian ethics and has been a source of inspiration for countless people throughout history.

MATTHEW

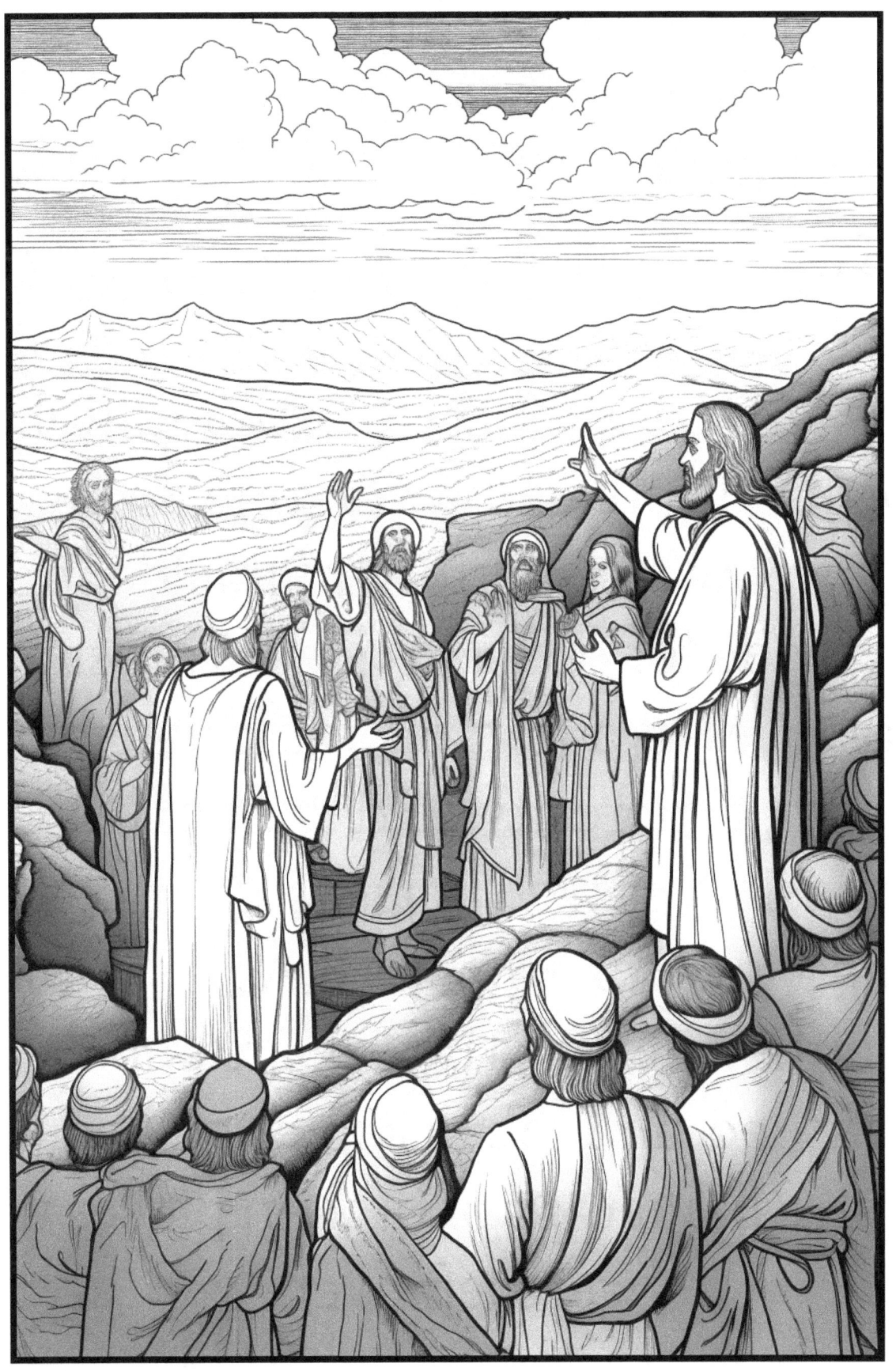

The feeding of the 5,000 is a miraculous story found in the Gospel of Matthew 14:13-21, where Jesus feeds a large crowd of people with just five loaves of bread and two fish. Despite the limited resources, Jesus multiplies the food and feeds everyone, showing his power to perform miracles and provide for those in need. This story teaches us about the importance of faith, generosity, and trust in God's provision, as well as Jesus' compassion and love for humanity. As it says in Matthew 14:20, "They all ate and were satisfied, and the disciples picked up twelve basketfuls of broken pieces that were left over."

MARK

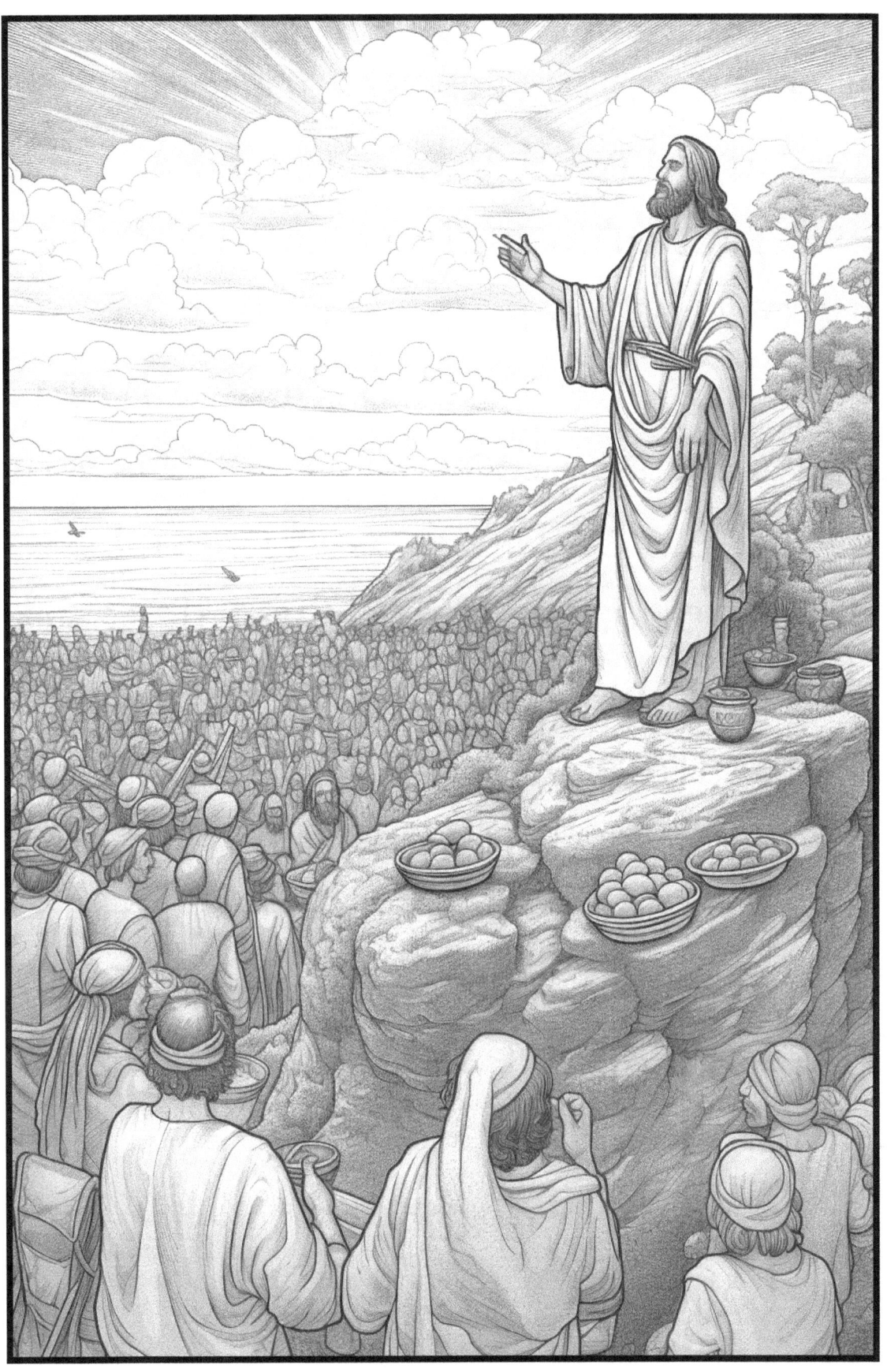

According to the Gospel of Luke, Jesus' resurrection from his tomb occurred on the third day after his crucifixion. The resurrection was first discovered by a group of women, including Mary Magdalene, who found the tomb empty and were greeted by two angels who told them that Jesus had risen. Jesus then appeared to his disciples and others, showing them his wounds and teaching them about the Scriptures. The resurrection is a central tenet of Christian faith, symbolizing the power of God over death and the promise of eternal life. The resurrection is a testament to the divinity of Jesus, and a source of hope and inspiration for believers around the world.

LUKE

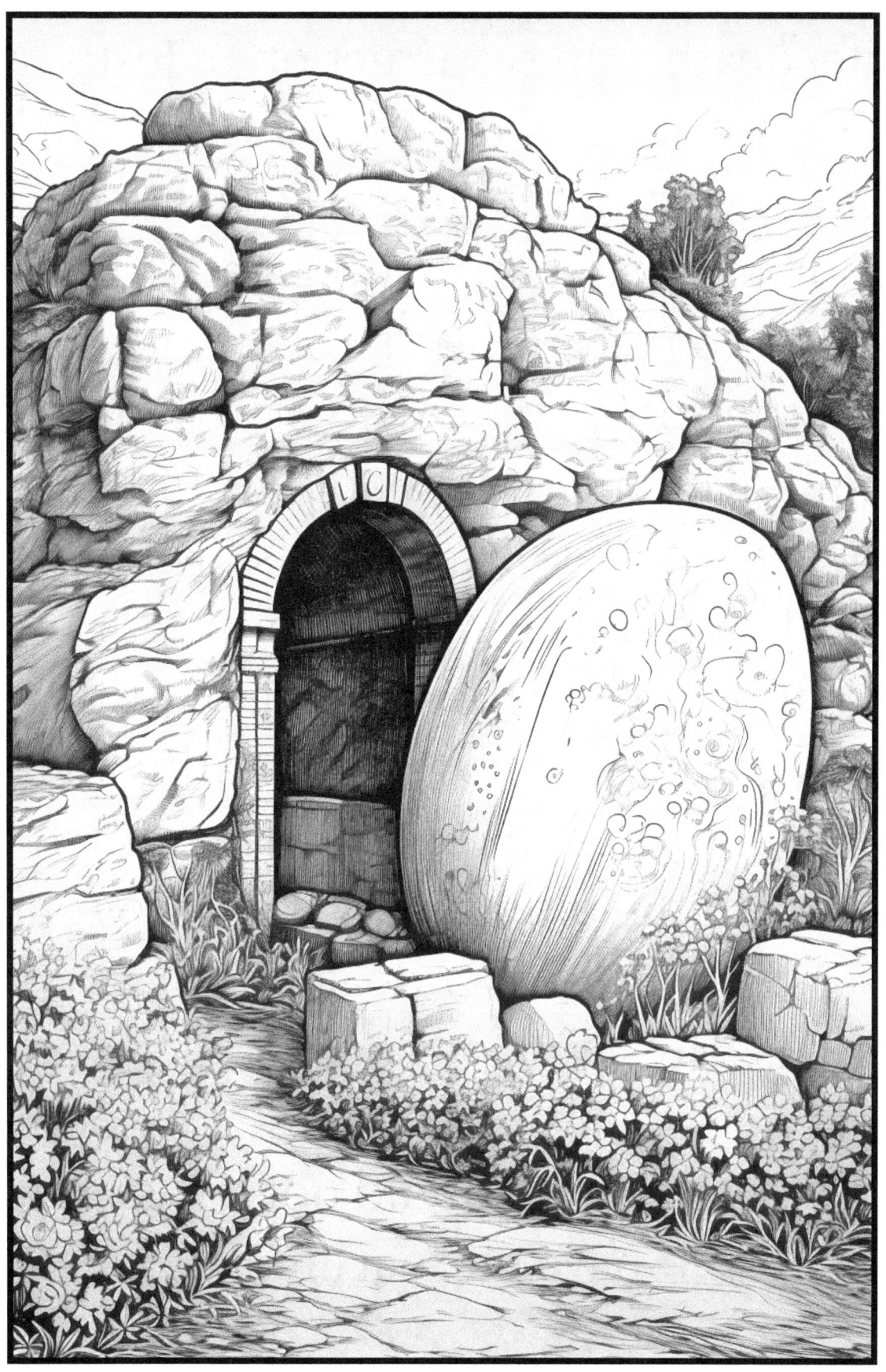

Life, death, and resurrection of Jesus, we learn that Jesus is the Son of God, sent by God the Father to give eternal life to all who believe in him. Who comes to earth as a Jew to restore God's covenant people. Yet the very people who ought to have embraced their Messiah rejected him: "He came to his own, and his own people did not receive him" (John 1:11).

John conveys the essence of Jesus' message and mission, culminating in the crucifixion and resurrection, which represent the ultimate victory of love and life over death.

John is 3:16 " For God so loved the world, that he gave his only Son, that whoever believes in him should not perish but have eternal life."

JOHN

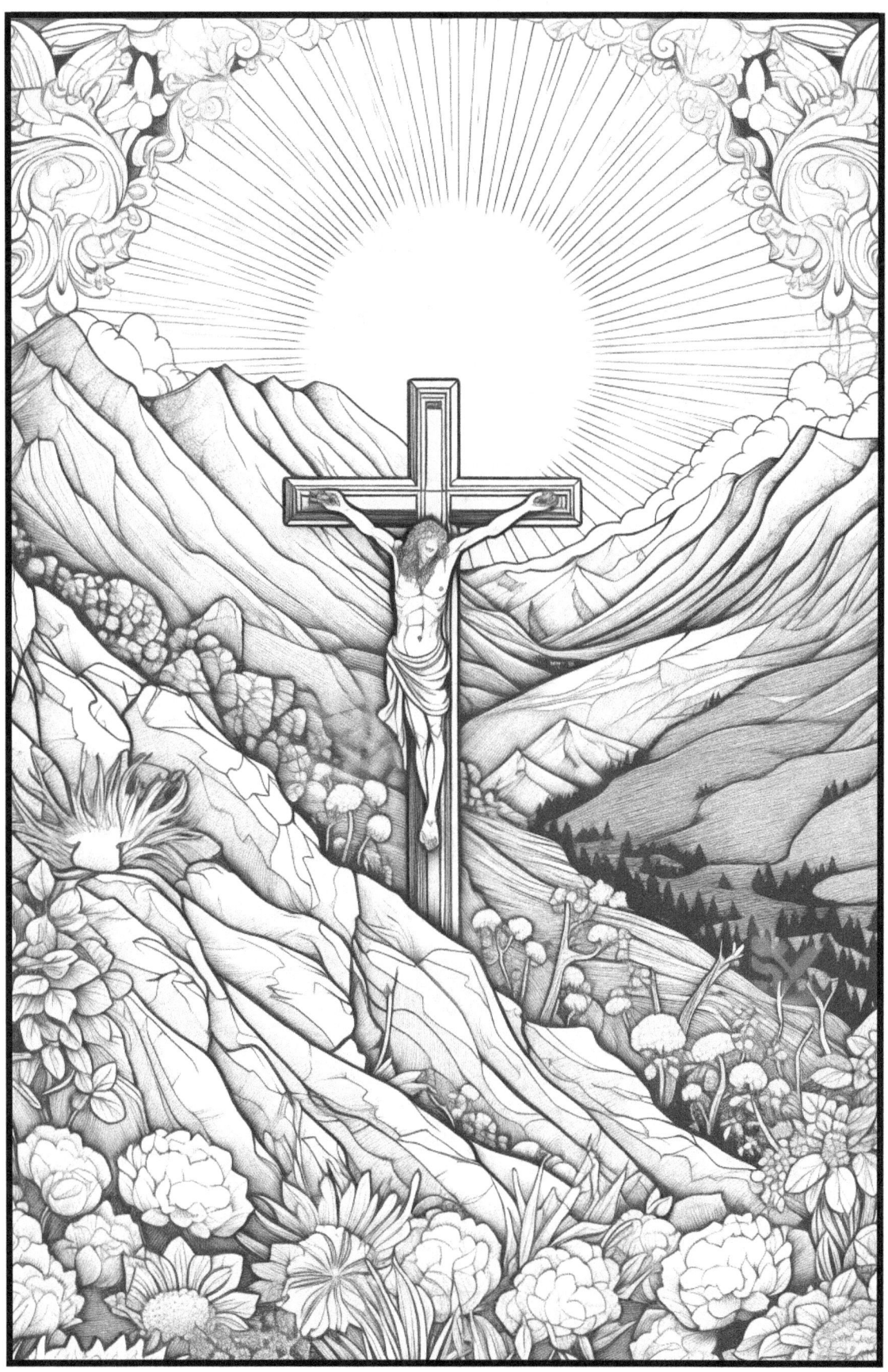

The Book of Acts is an account of the birth and growth of Christianity, chronicling the spread of the gospel message and the establishment of the early Christian church. Through the work of the apostles and the power of the Holy Spirit, the message of salvation is shared with people of all nations and cultures, leading to the formation of new churches and the growth of the Christian movement.

A key verse from the Book of Acts is Acts 1:8, which reads: "But you will receive power when the Holy Spirit comes on you; and you will be my witnesses in Jerusalem, and in all Judea and Samaria, and to the ends of the earth."

ACTS

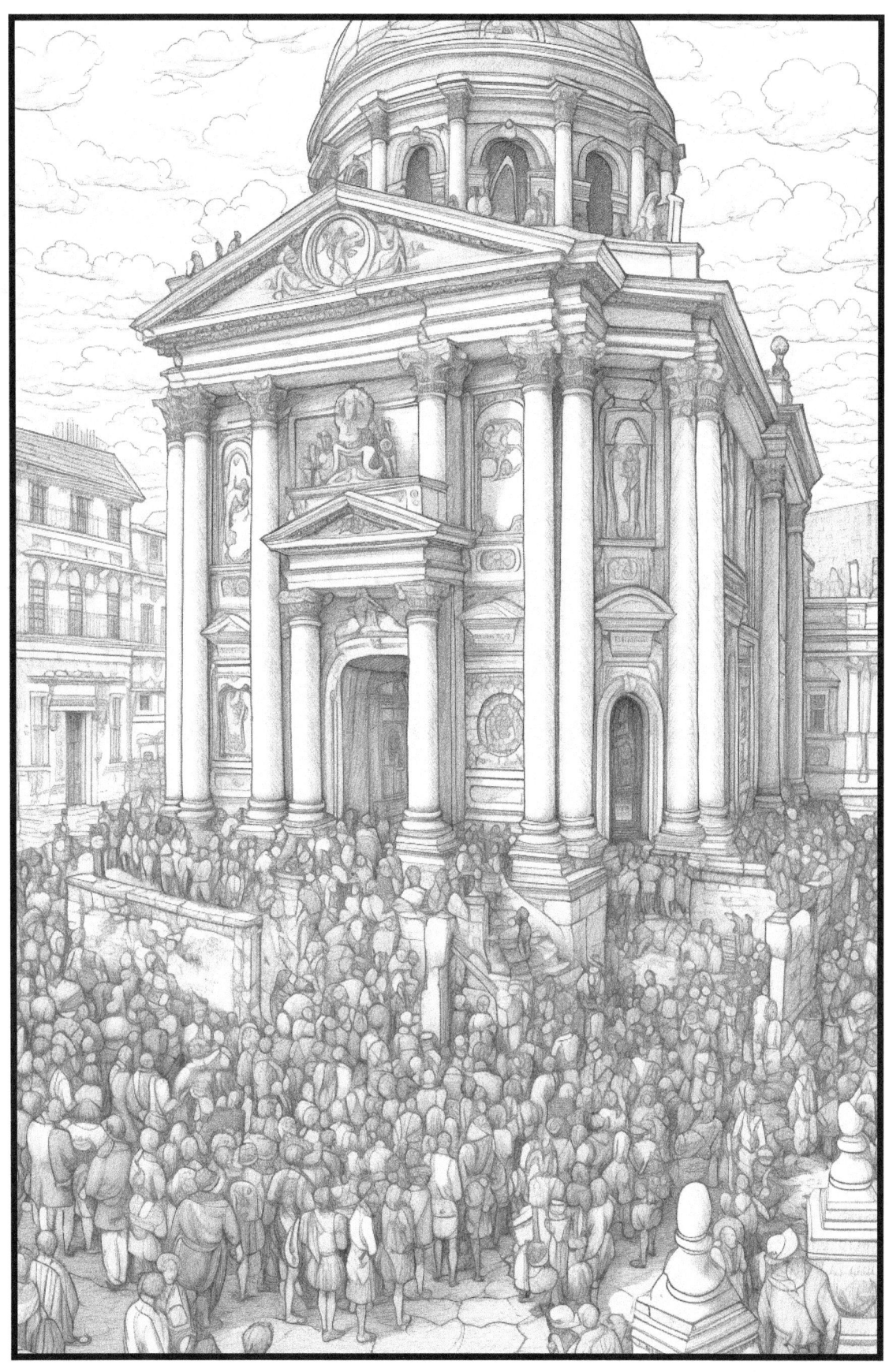

The Apostle Paul urges believers to live as lights in the darkness, shining the love and truth of Christ into the world around them. He writes in Romans 13:12, "The night is far gone; the day is at hand. So then let us cast off the works of darkness and put on the armor of light." The image of a torch represents this call to be a shining witness, illuminating the darkness and pointing the way to salvation. Paul emphasizes throughout the book of Romans the importance of living transformed lives, turning away from sin and living in righteousness and love. As Christians live out their faith in this way, they become beacons of hope in a dark and broken world.

ROMANS

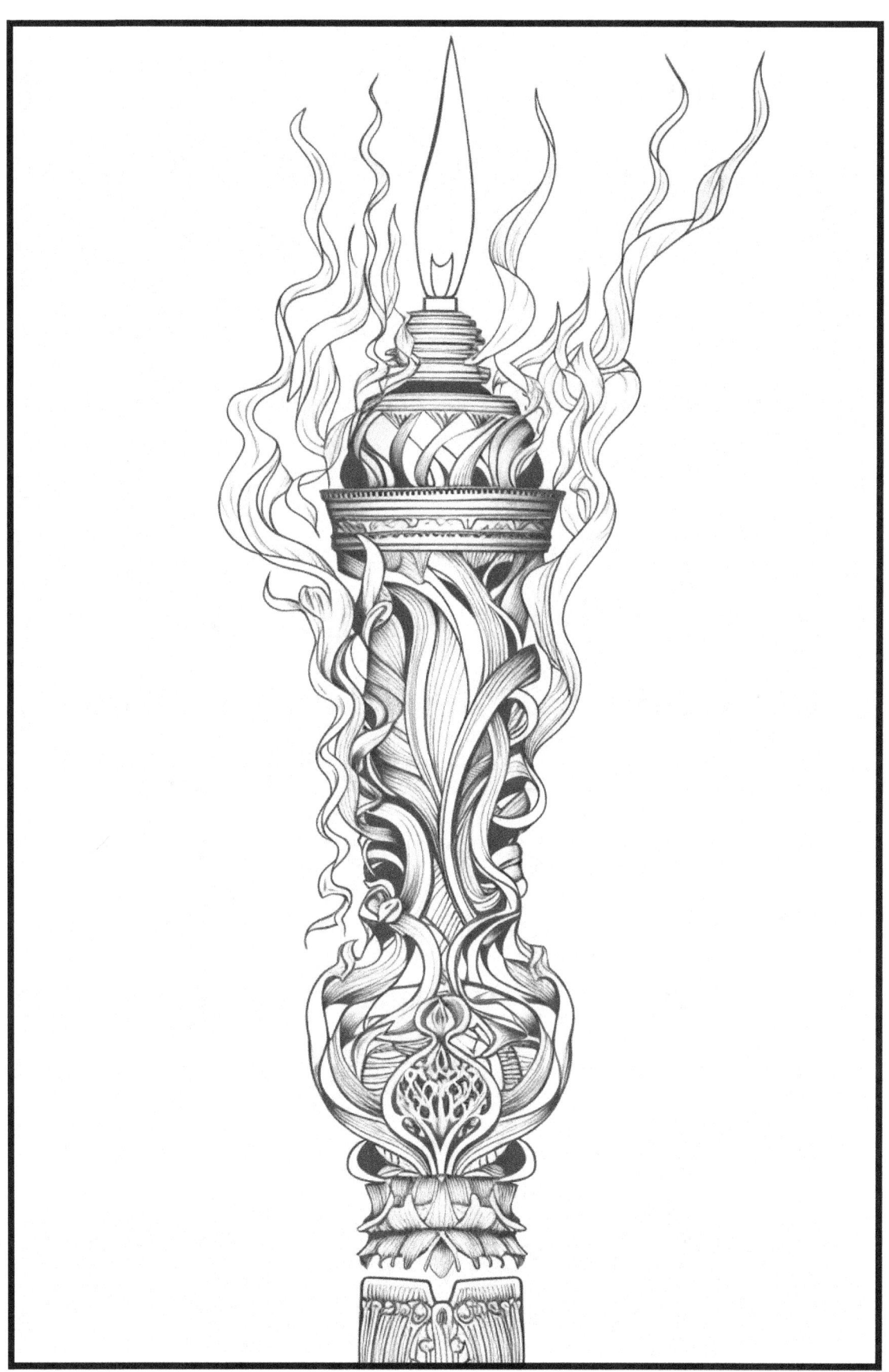

In 1 Corinthians 13, the apostle Paul provides a powerful and profound description of what love truly is. He explains that love is not just an emotion or feeling, but rather a steadfast commitment to others. Love endures all things, meaning that it doesn't falter or give up in the face of adversity or hardship. The verse "Love bears all things, believes all things, hopes all things, endures all things" 1 Corinthians 13:7 captures the enduring nature of love and the importance of holding on to it, no matter what challenges may come our way. This enduring love is what can sustain us through difficult times and bring us closer to those we love.

1 CORINTHIANS

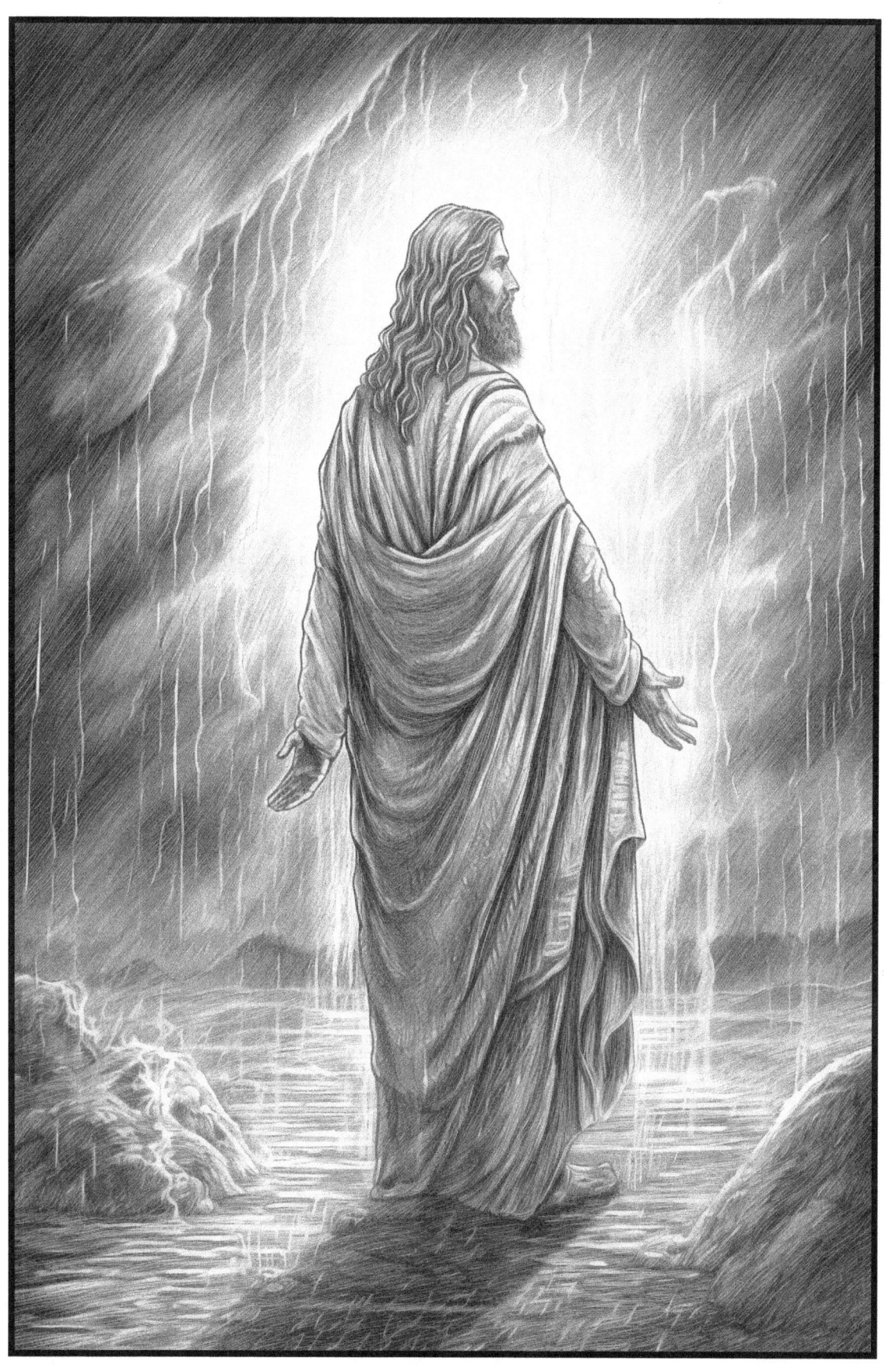

2 Corinthians emphasizes the comfort and strength that believers can find in God during their trials and afflictions. In 2 Corinthians 1:3-4, it says, "Blessed be the God and Father of our Lord Jesus Christ, the Father of mercies and God of all comfort, who comforts us in all our affliction, so that we may be able to comfort those who are in any affliction, with the comfort with which we ourselves are comforted by God." This verse portrays a person being comforted by God during their time of distress, with the idea that this comfort can then be passed on to others who may be going through similar struggles. This verse gives the comfort that God can provide in times of need.

2 CORINTHIANS

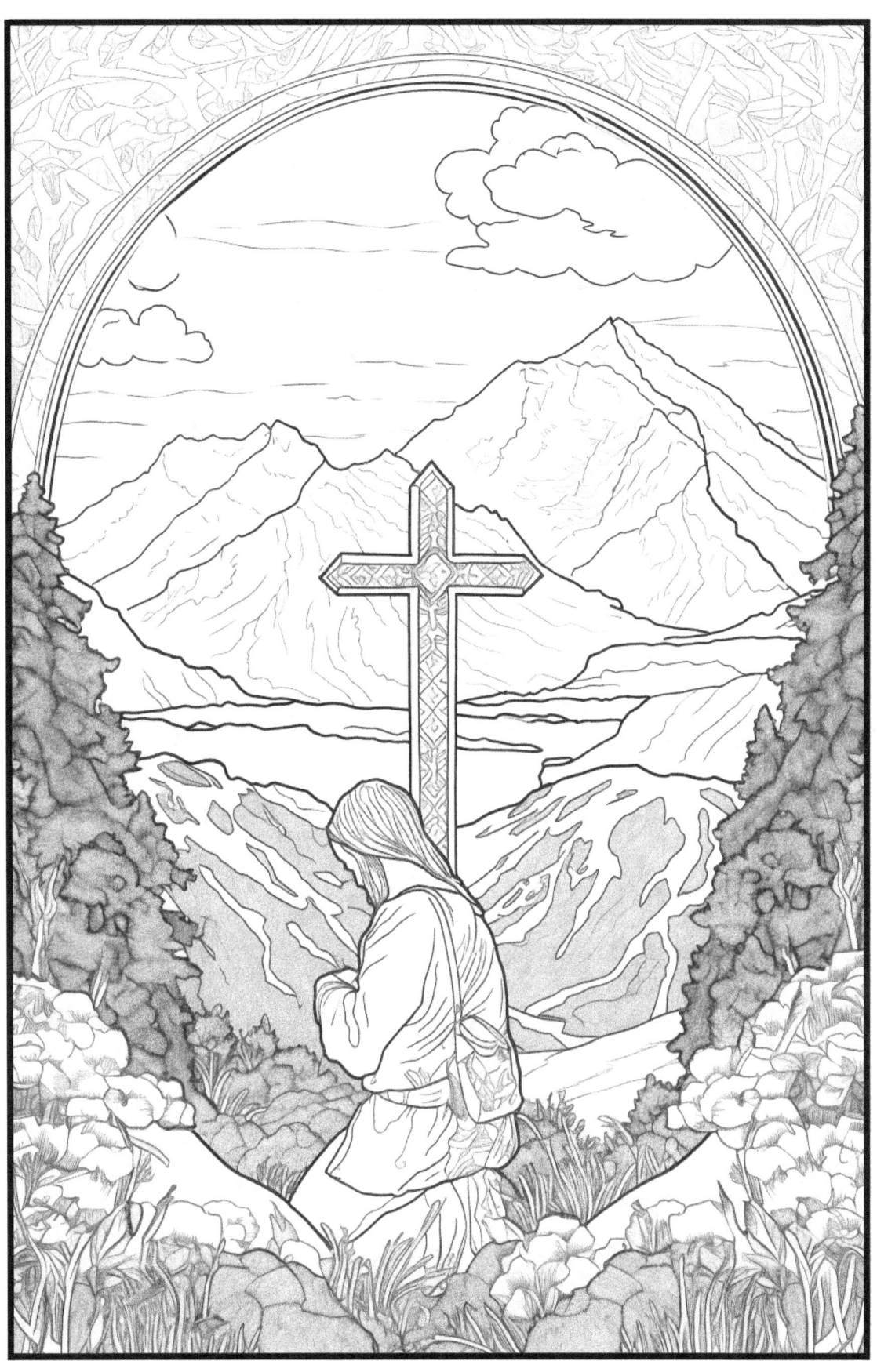

The concept of freedom is discussed in the context of being freed from the law and legalism, and instead embracing faith in Jesus Christ as the basis for salvation. The apostle Paul writes in Galatians 5:1, "For freedom Christ has set us free; stand firm therefore, and do not submit again to a yoke of slavery." This means that through faith in Jesus, believers are freed from the burden of trying to earn their salvation through adherence to the law, and instead can live in the freedom of grace. Therefore, the freedom found in Christ is not a license to do whatever one pleases, but rather an opportunity to live in love and service to others.

GALATIANS

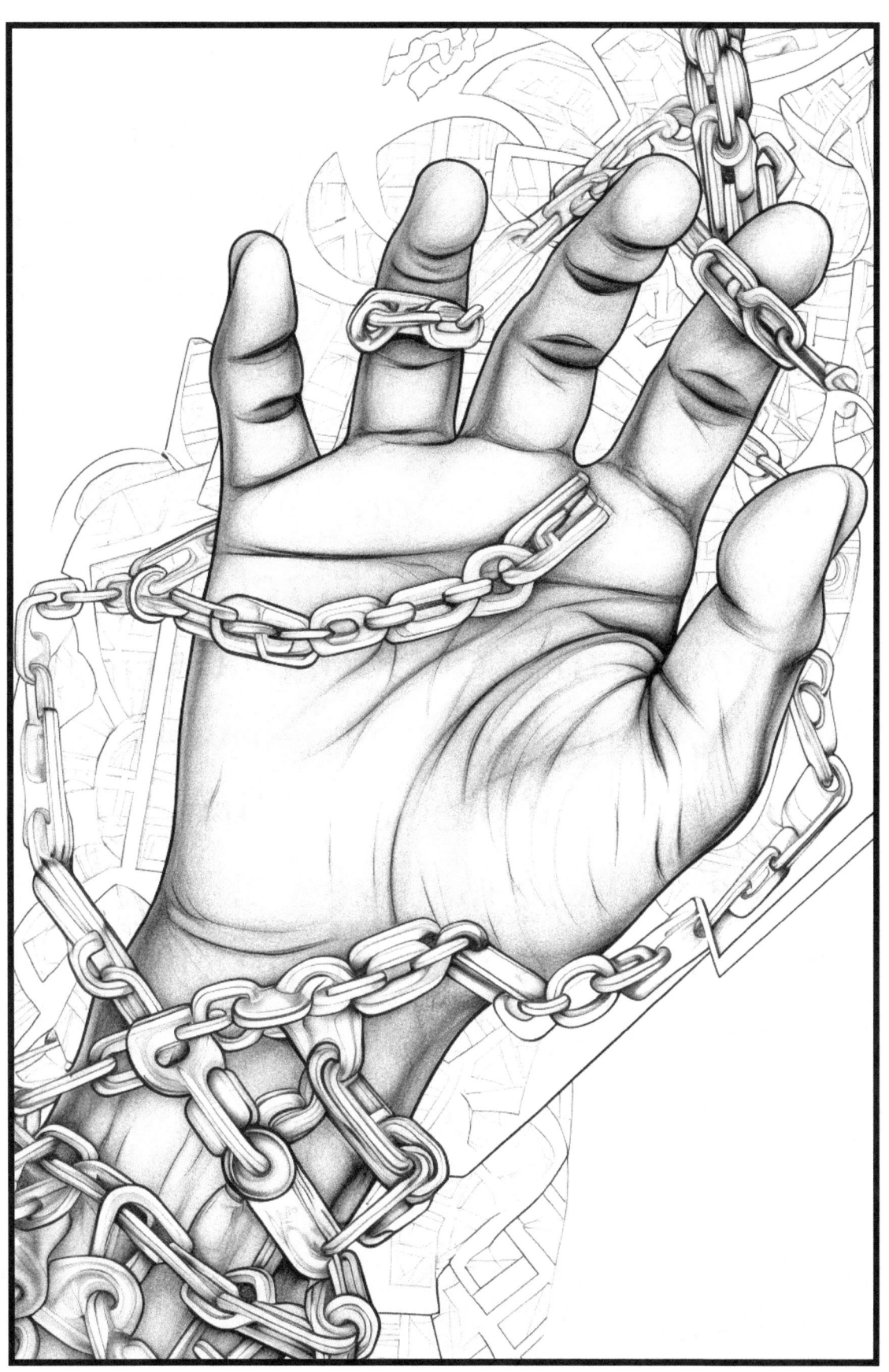

Ephesians 6:10-18, the apostle Paul exhorts believers to put on the full armor of God to stand against the schemes of the devil. Full armor can represent the spiritual warfare that believers must engage in, and the armor of God that they can put on for protection and strength. As Paul writes in Ephesians 6:13-14, "Therefore take up the whole armor of God, that you may be able to withstand in the evil day, and having done all, to stand firm. Stand therefore, having fastened on the belt of truth, and having put on the breastplate of righteousness." This emphasizes the importance of being equipped with the truth, righteousness, faith, salvation, and the word of God to withstand the attacks of the enemy.

EPHESIANS

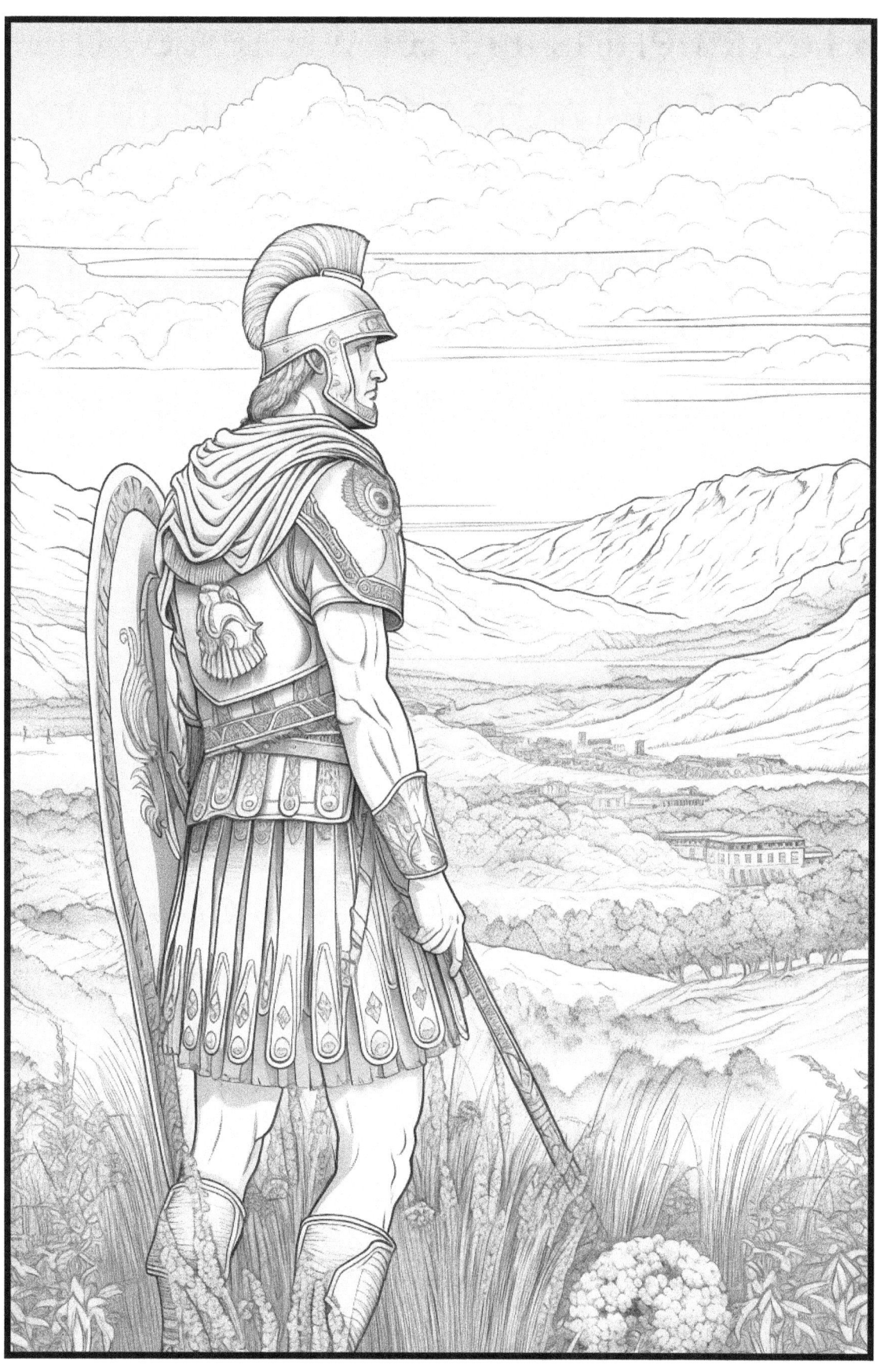

The book of Philippians in the New Testament is a letter written by the apostle Paul to the church in Philippi. It conveys a message of joy and encouragement despite Paul's own imprisonment. The book emphasizes the importance of unity, humility, and having a mindset focused on Christ. It encourages believers to rejoice in all circumstances and to find their strength in Christ alone. As Paul writes in Philippians 2:2-3, "Complete my joy by being of the same mind, having the same love, being in full accord and of one mind. Do nothing from selfish ambition or conceit, but in humility count others more significant than yourselves." This verse encapsulates the call to unity, selflessness, and humility that permeates the book of Philippians.

PILLIPIANS

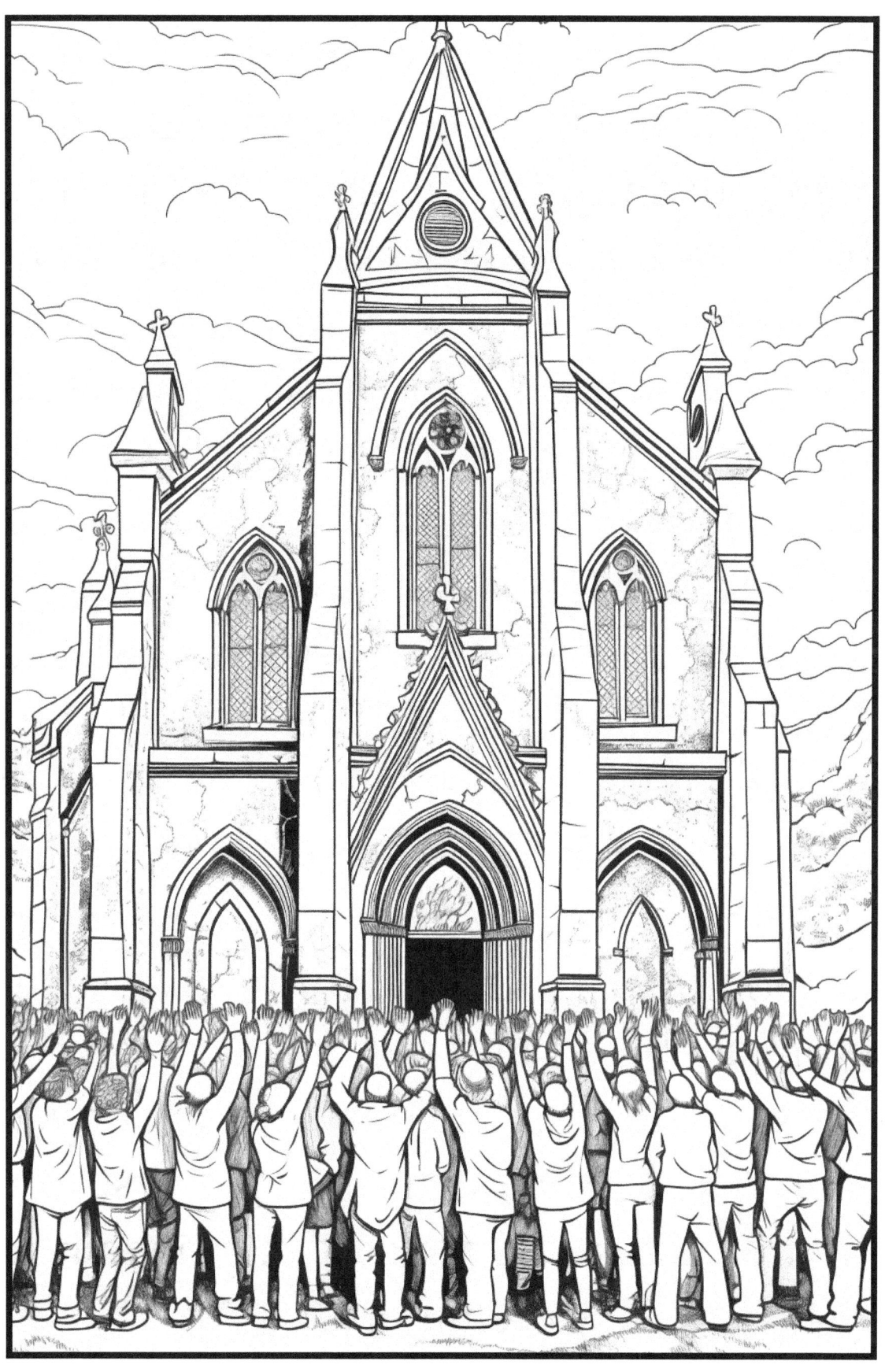

The book of Colossians in the New Testament is a letter written by the apostle Paul to the church in Colossae. It emphasizes the preeminence and sufficiency of Christ in all things. Paul addresses false teachings and urges believers to hold fast to the truth of the Gospel. He highlights the supremacy of Christ as the image of the invisible God, the firstborn over all creation, and the head of the Church. In Colossians 1:15-18, Paul writes, "He is the image of the invisible God, the firstborn of all creation. For by him all things were created, in heaven and on earth, visible and invisible, whether thrones or dominions or rulers or authorities—all things were created through him and for him. And he is before all things, and in him all things hold together. And he is the head of the body, the church. He is the beginning, the firstborn from the dead, that in everything he might be preeminent."

COLOSSIANS

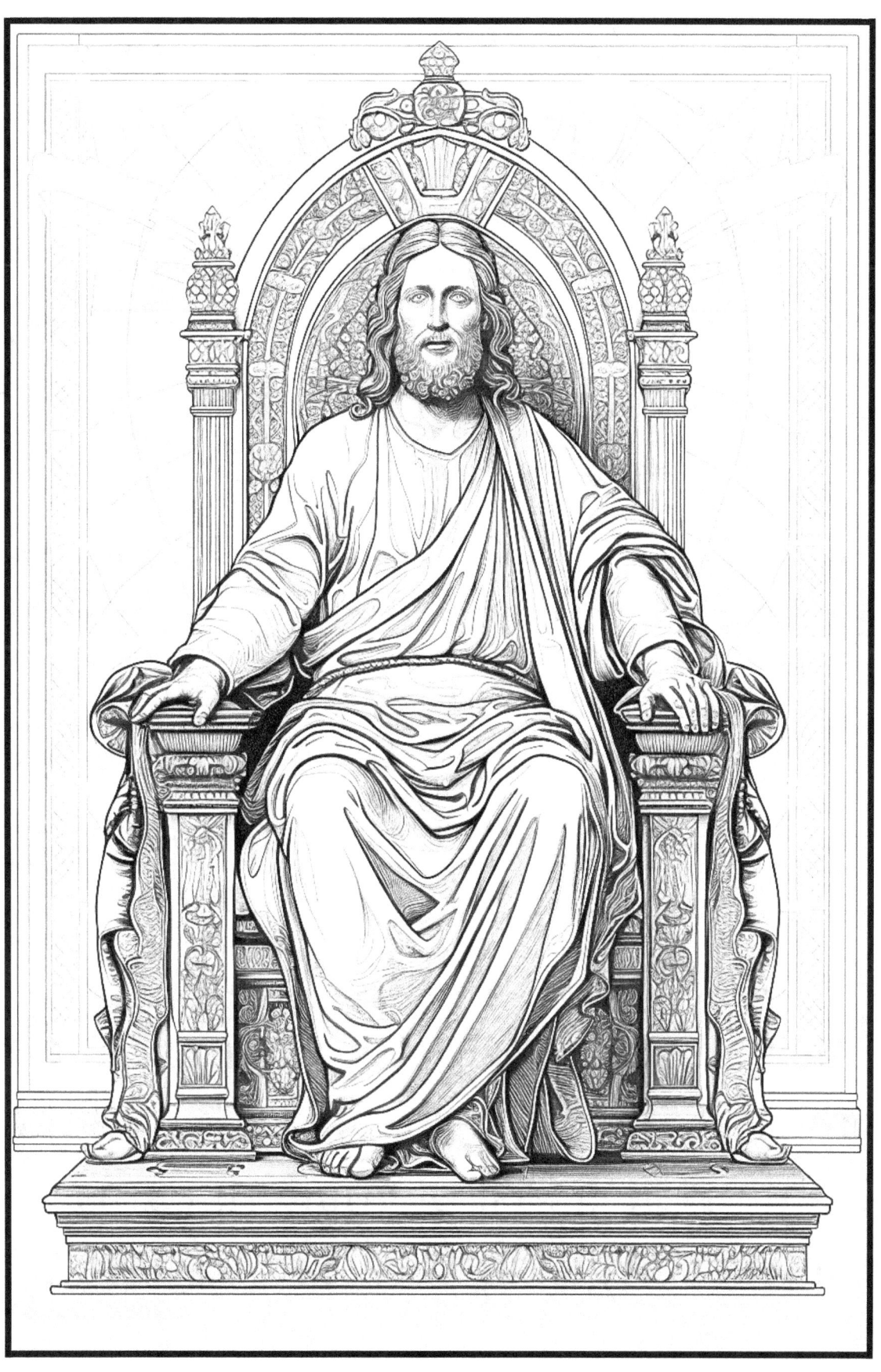

The book of Thessalonians in the New Testament consists of two letters written by the apostle Paul to the church in Thessalonica. It addresses various topics including the second coming of Christ, the importance of holy living, and the hope of resurrection. The letters encourage and instruct believers in their faith, urging them to remain steadfast and be prepared for Christ's return.

In 1 Thessalonians 5:16-18, Paul writes, "Rejoice always, pray without ceasing, give thanks in all circumstances; for this is the will of God in Christ Jesus for you." This verse encapsulates the message of living a joyful, prayerful, and thankful life, even in the midst of challenges, as we await the glorious return of Christ.

THESSALONIANS

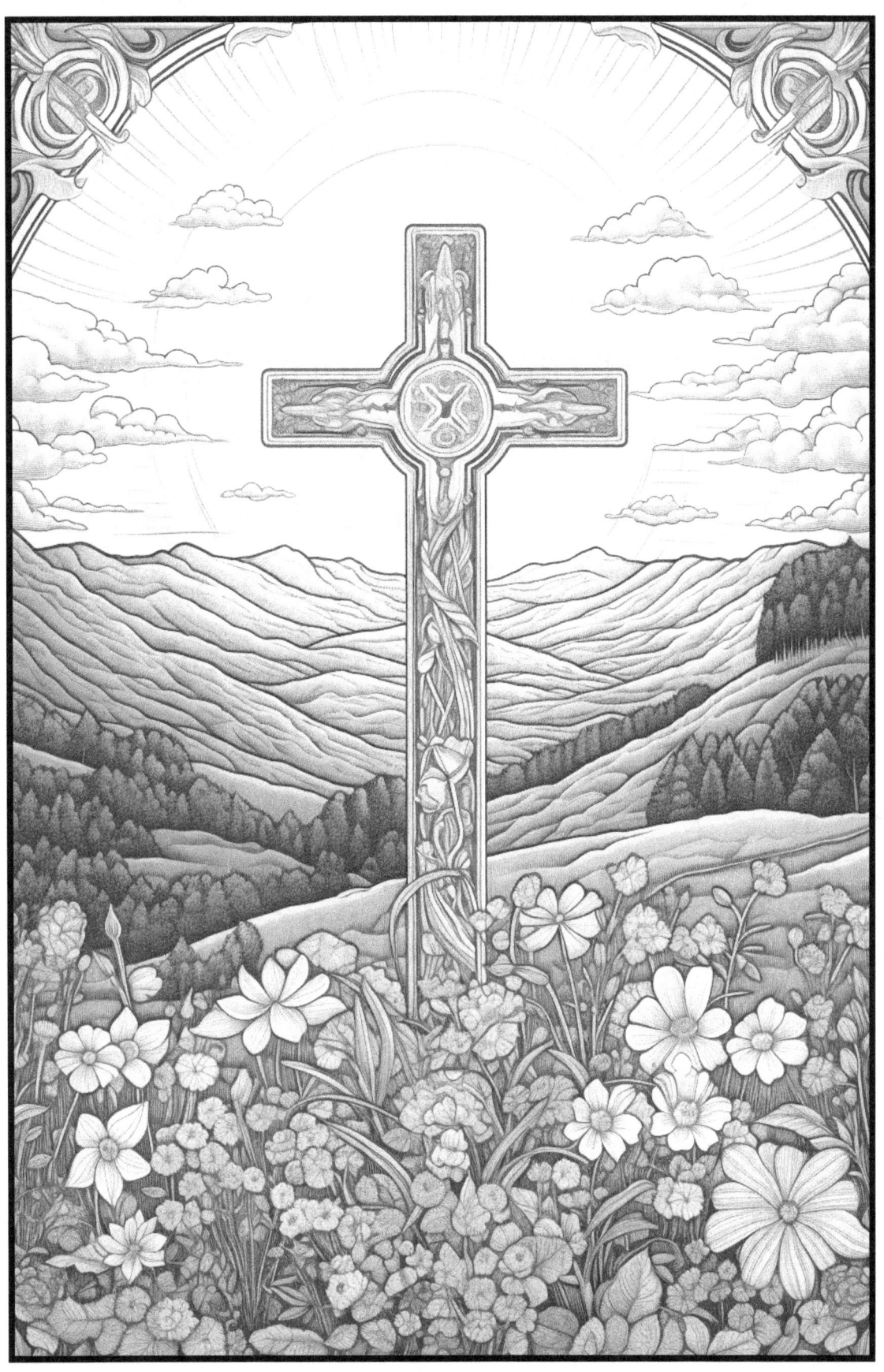

The book of Timothy in the New Testament consists of two letters written by the apostle Paul to his protégé Timothy, who was a young leader in the early Christian church. These letters provide practical guidance and instruction for Timothy's ministry and the church at large. They address topics such as leadership, false teachings, sound doctrine, and personal conduct.

In 1 Timothy 4:12, Paul writes, "Let no one despise you for your youth, but set the believers an example in speech, in conduct, in love, in faith, in purity." This verse encapsulates the message of Timothy, encouraging young leaders to embrace their calling and lead by example, demonstrating godly character and commitment to the faith.

1-2 TIMOTHY

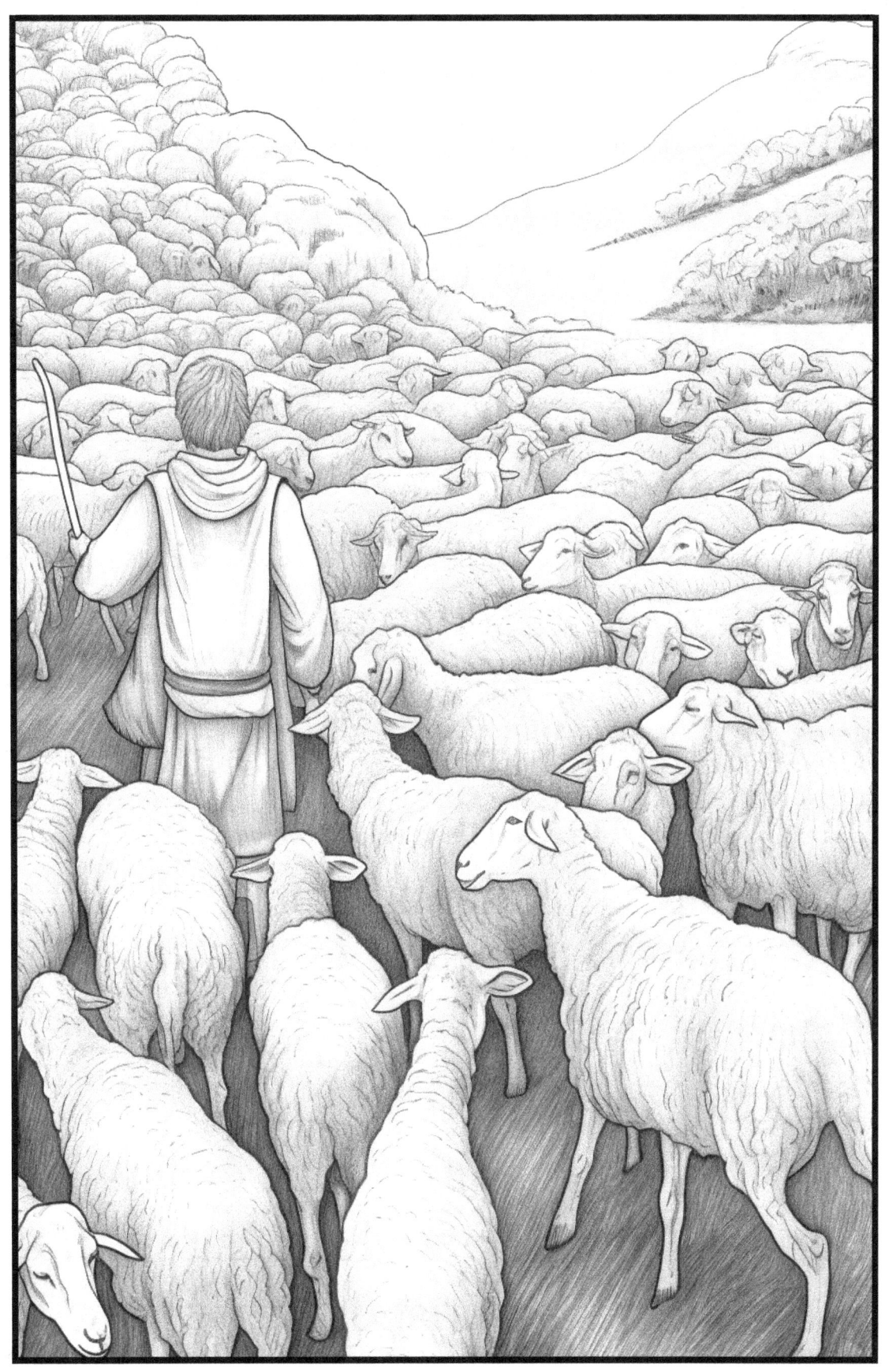

The book of Titus in the New Testament is a letter written by the apostle Paul to his trusted companion Titus. This letter provides guidance for leading and organizing the church in the island of Crete. It emphasizes the importance of sound doctrine, righteous living, and maintaining good works within the Christian community. In Titus 2:7-8, Paul writes, "Show yourself in all respects to be a model of good works, and in your teaching show integrity, dignity, and sound speech that cannot be condemned." This quote encapsulates the message of Titus, urging believers to live lives of exemplary character, demonstrating integrity, and speaking in a way that honors God. A lighthouse, symbolizing the call to be a shining example of righteousness and integrity in the midst of a dark world.

TITUS

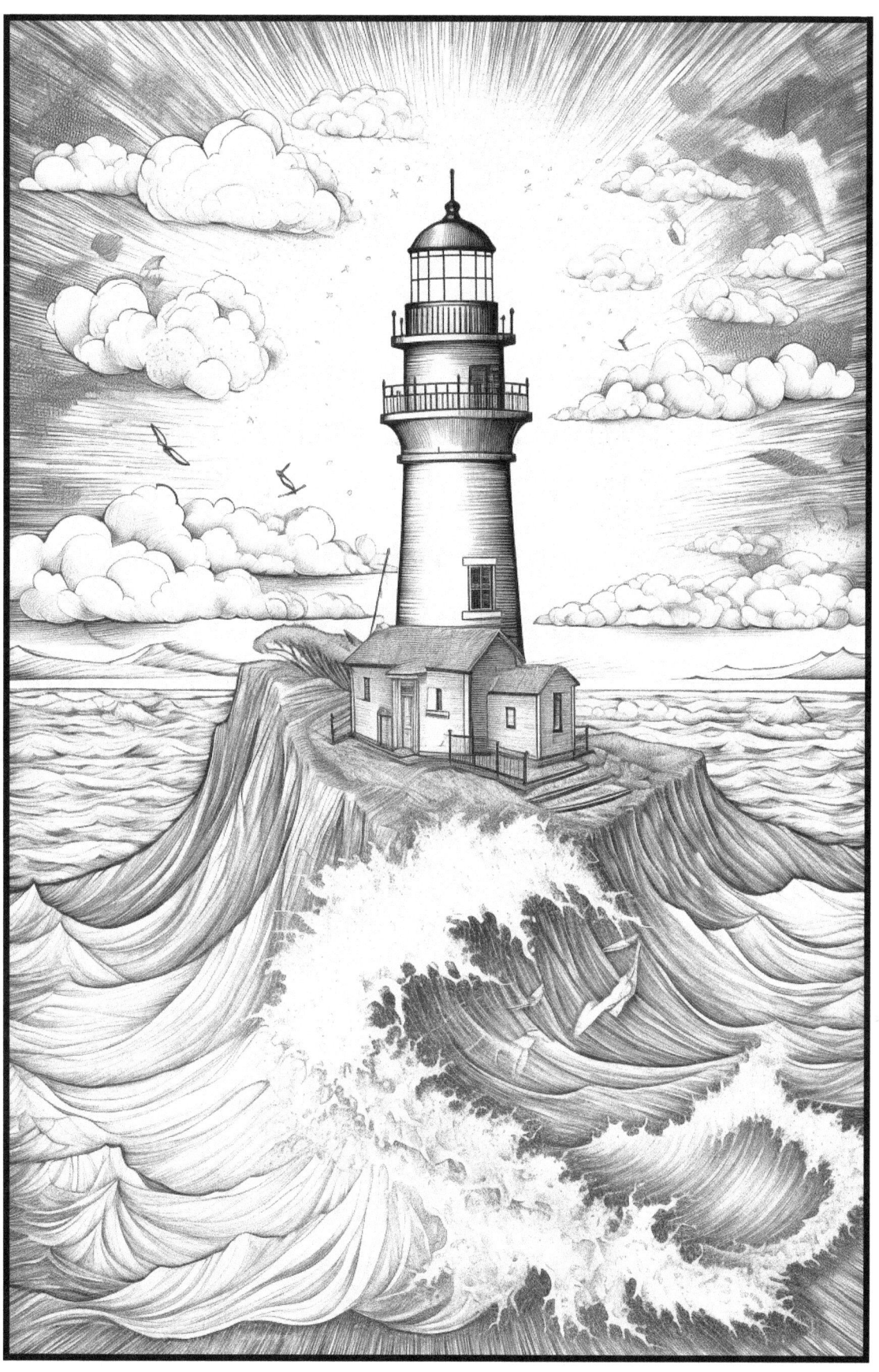

The book of Philemon in the New Testament is a personal letter written by the apostle Paul to Philemon, a Christian slave owner. The letter appeals to Philemon to receive his runaway slave, Onesimus, not as a slave but as a beloved brother in Christ. It highlights the power of forgiveness, reconciliation, and the transformative nature of the Gospel. In Philemon 1:15-16, Paul writes, "Perhaps the reason he was separated from you for a little while was that you might have him back forever —no longer as a slave, but better than a slave, as a dear brother. He is very dear to me but even dearer to you, both as a fellow man and as a brother in the Lord." This quote encapsulates the message of Philemon, urging believers to embrace the spirit of forgiveness, love, and equality in Christ, transcending social and cultural boundaries. Forgiveness between Philemon and Onesimus, depicting the restoration of their relationship through forgiveness and reconciliation.

PHILEMON

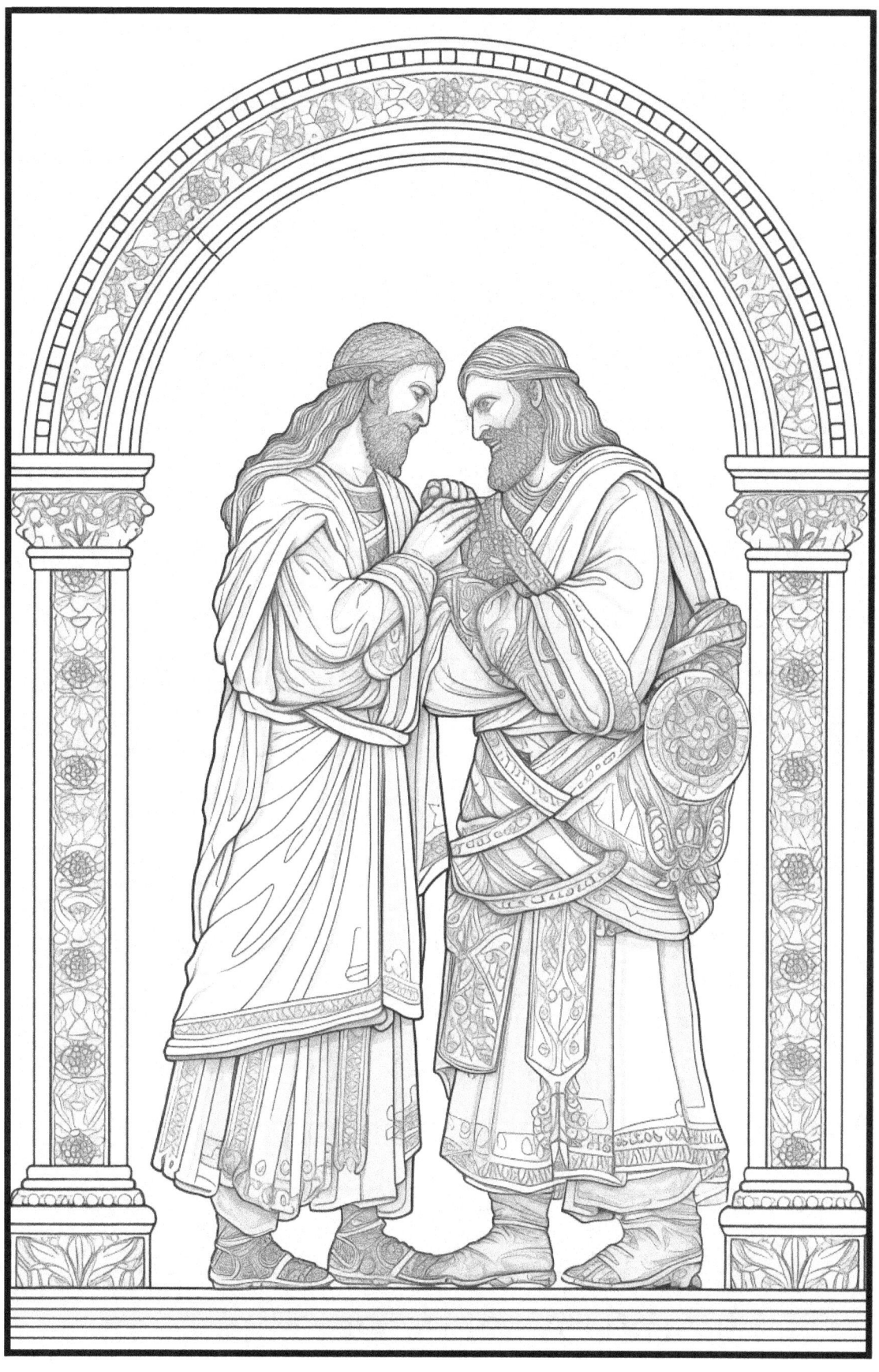

The book of Hebrews is a rich and profound exploration of the superiority of Jesus Christ and the new covenant He established. It emphasizes the supremacy of Christ over the Old Testament laws, rituals, and sacrifices, pointing to His role as the ultimate High Priest and the perfect mediator between God and humanity. The book encourages believers to persevere in their faith and to hold fast to the hope found in Jesus. Hebrews 12:2 encapsulates this message, saying, "fixing our eyes on Jesus, the pioneer and perfecter of faith. For the joy set before him he endured the cross, scorning its shame, and sat down at the right hand of the throne of God." This quote highlights the centrality of Christ and His redemptive work, calling believers to focus their attention and devotion on Him as the source of true faith and eternal hope. Crown of thorns, symbolizing Jesus as the pioneer and perfecter of faith, who endured the cross and scorned its shame for the joy set before Him.

HEBREWS

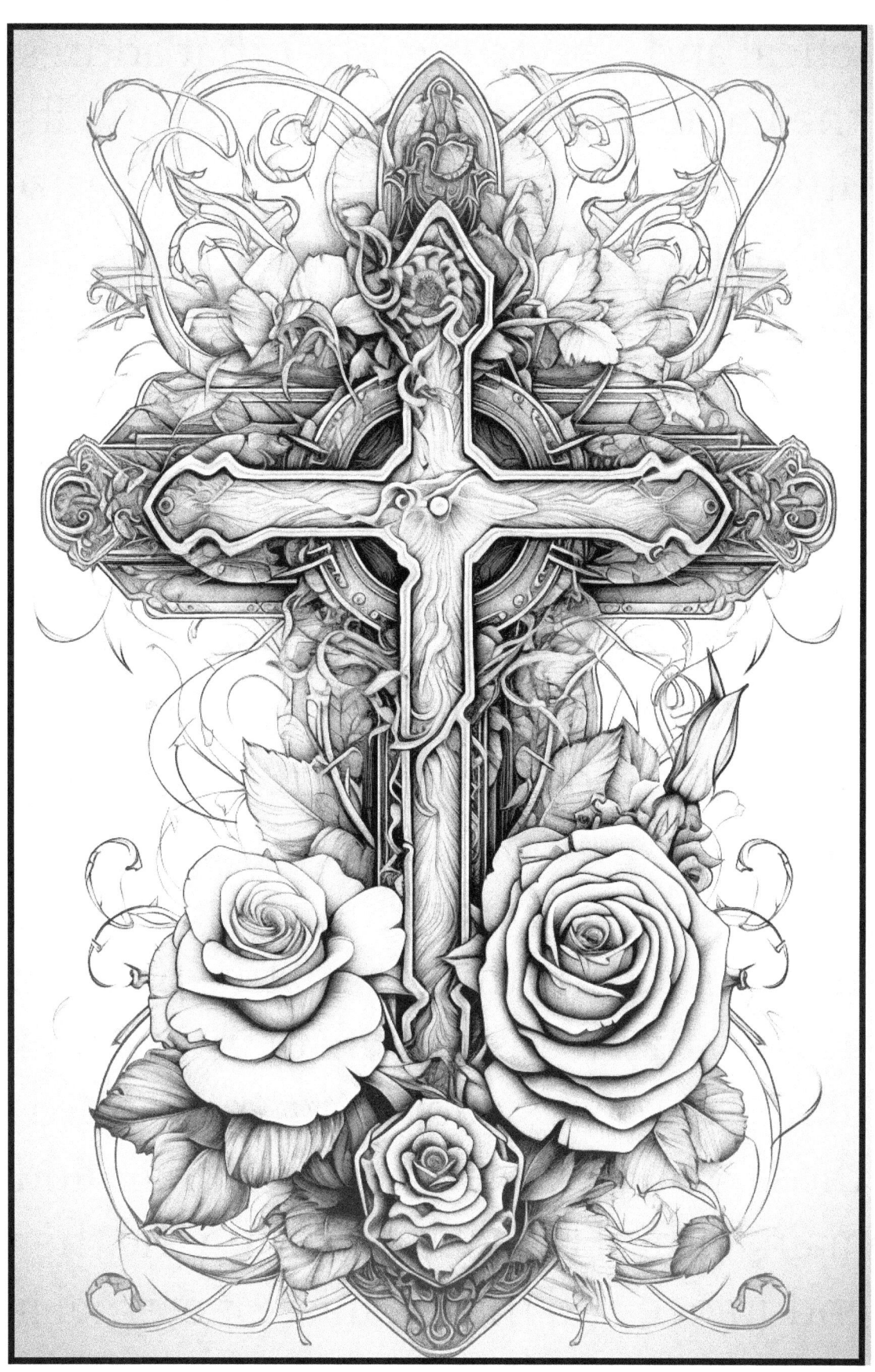

The book of James in the New Testament is a practical and convicting letter that addresses the importance of genuine faith and its outworking in everyday life. It emphasizes the need for believers to live out their faith through good works, demonstrating the authenticity of their relationship with God. James 1:22 encapsulates this message, stating, "But be doers of the word, and not hearers only, deceiving yourselves." This quote highlights the call to action and the importance of aligning one's actions with the teachings of God's Word. James challenges believers to demonstrate their faith through acts of compassion, love, and righteousness, emphasizing the transformative power of true faith that leads to a life of integrity and godliness. Crown symbolizing the reward for those who persevere through trials and remain faithful to God, capturing the theme of endurance and the promise of eternal life.

JAMES

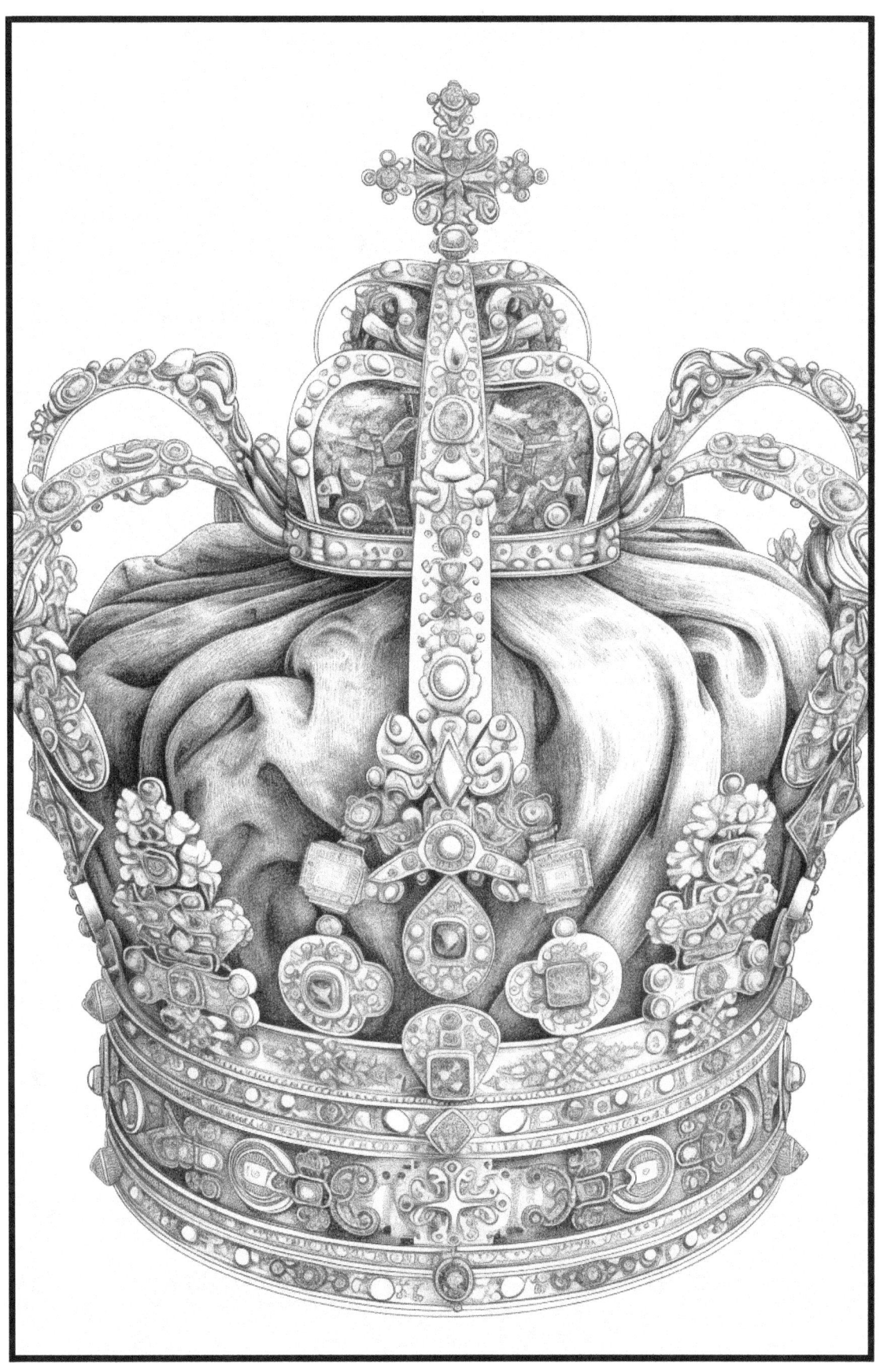

The book of 1 Peter in the New Testament is a letter written by the apostle Peter to encourage and strengthen persecuted believers. It addresses various themes such as suffering, hope, and living as a witness for Christ in a hostile world. Peter emphasizes the believers' identity as a chosen people and urges them to live holy lives that reflect the character of God. 1 Peter 2:9 captures this message, stating, "But you are a chosen race, a royal priesthood, a holy nation, a people for his own possession, that you may proclaim the excellencies of him who called you out of darkness into his marvelous light." This quote highlights the believers' special position as God's chosen people, called to proclaim His praises and live in a way that reflects His glorious light.

1 PETER

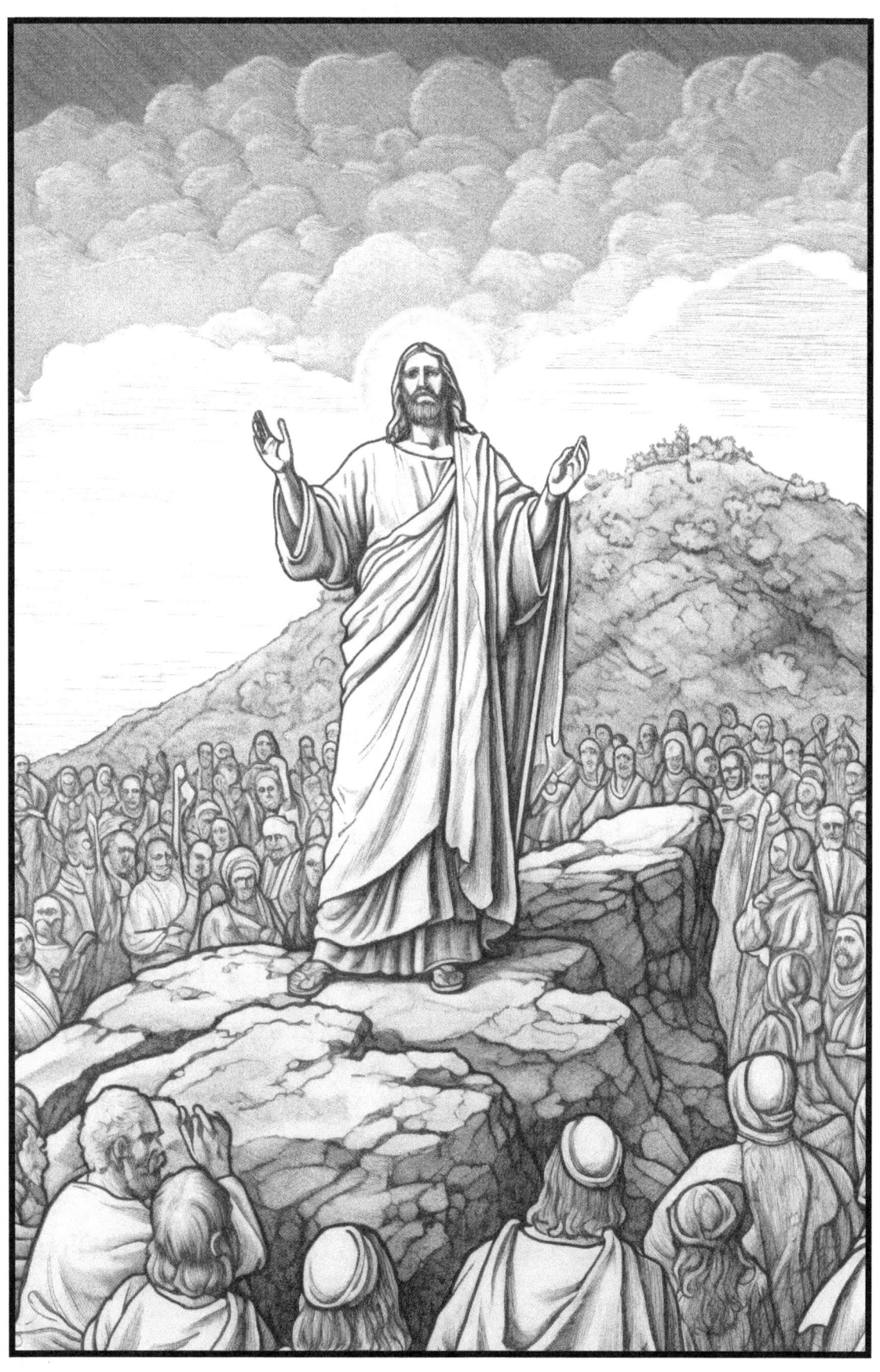

The book of 2 Peter highlights the significance of knowledge, virtue, and the steadfast hope in the second coming of Christ. Peter encourages believers to continually grow in the grace and knowledge of our Lord and Savior Jesus Christ, reminding them that through this growth, they can navigate the challenges of false teachings and confidently anticipate the glorious future promised by God. In 2 Peter 3:18, he writes, "But grow in the grace and knowledge of our Lord and Savior Jesus Christ. To him be the glory both now and to the day of eternity. Amen." Signifying the importance of knowledge and spiritual growth, the open book represents the pursuit of understanding God's Word, while the growing plant represents the continuous development and maturity of faith.

2 PETER

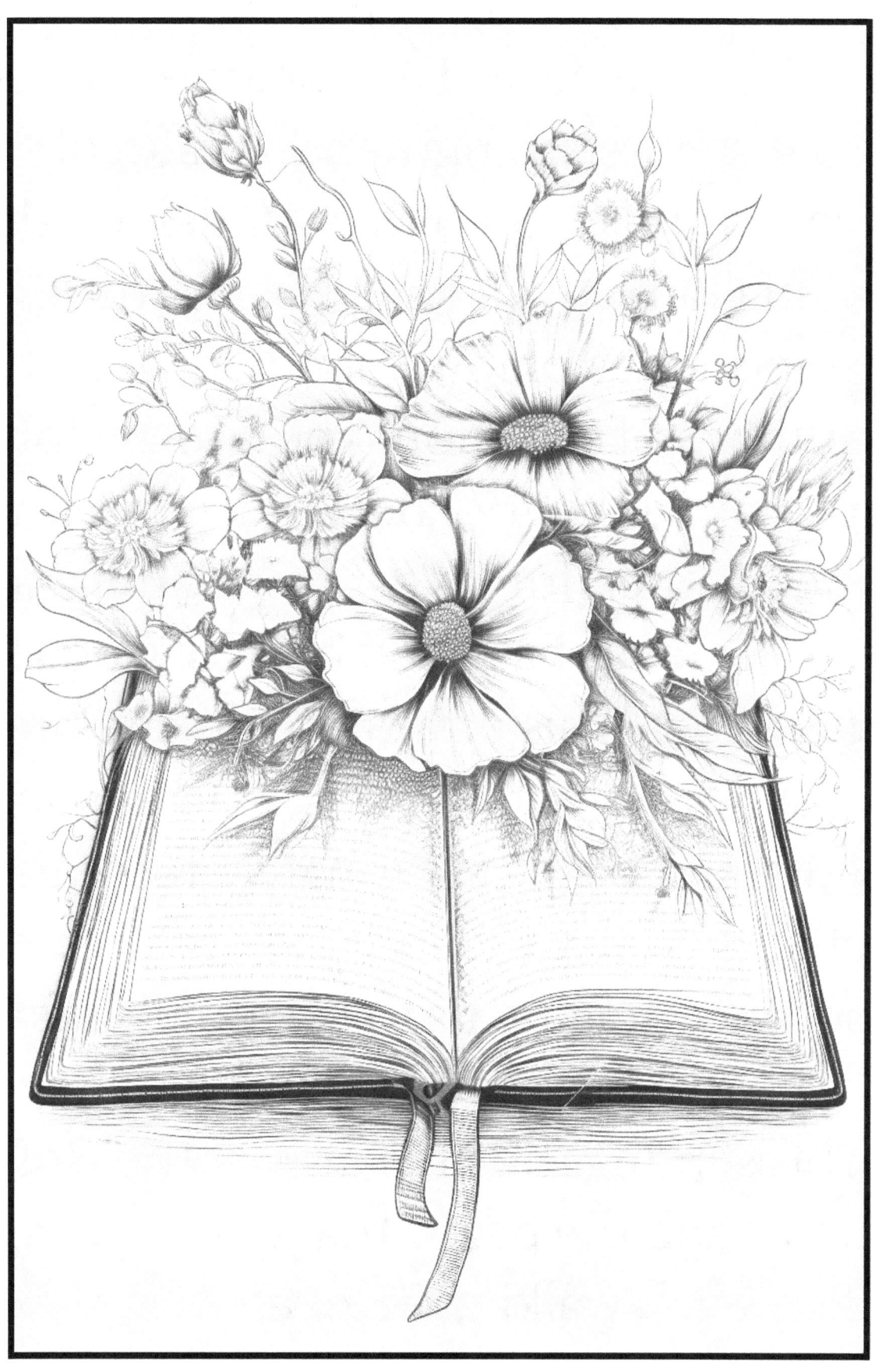

The book of 1 John in the New Testament can be summarized as a heartfelt letter written to strengthen the faith of believers and deepen their understanding of God's love. It emphasizes the importance of love, obedience, and assurance of salvation. The apostle John writes in 1 John 4:7, "Beloved, let us love one another, for love is from God, and whoever loves has been born of God and knows God." This powerful verse reminds us that love is not only a characteristic of God but also a transformative force that reflects our true identity as children of God, encouraging us to live out our faith in love for one another. A dove, representing the presence of the Holy Spirit and the peace that comes from walking in love.

1 JOHN

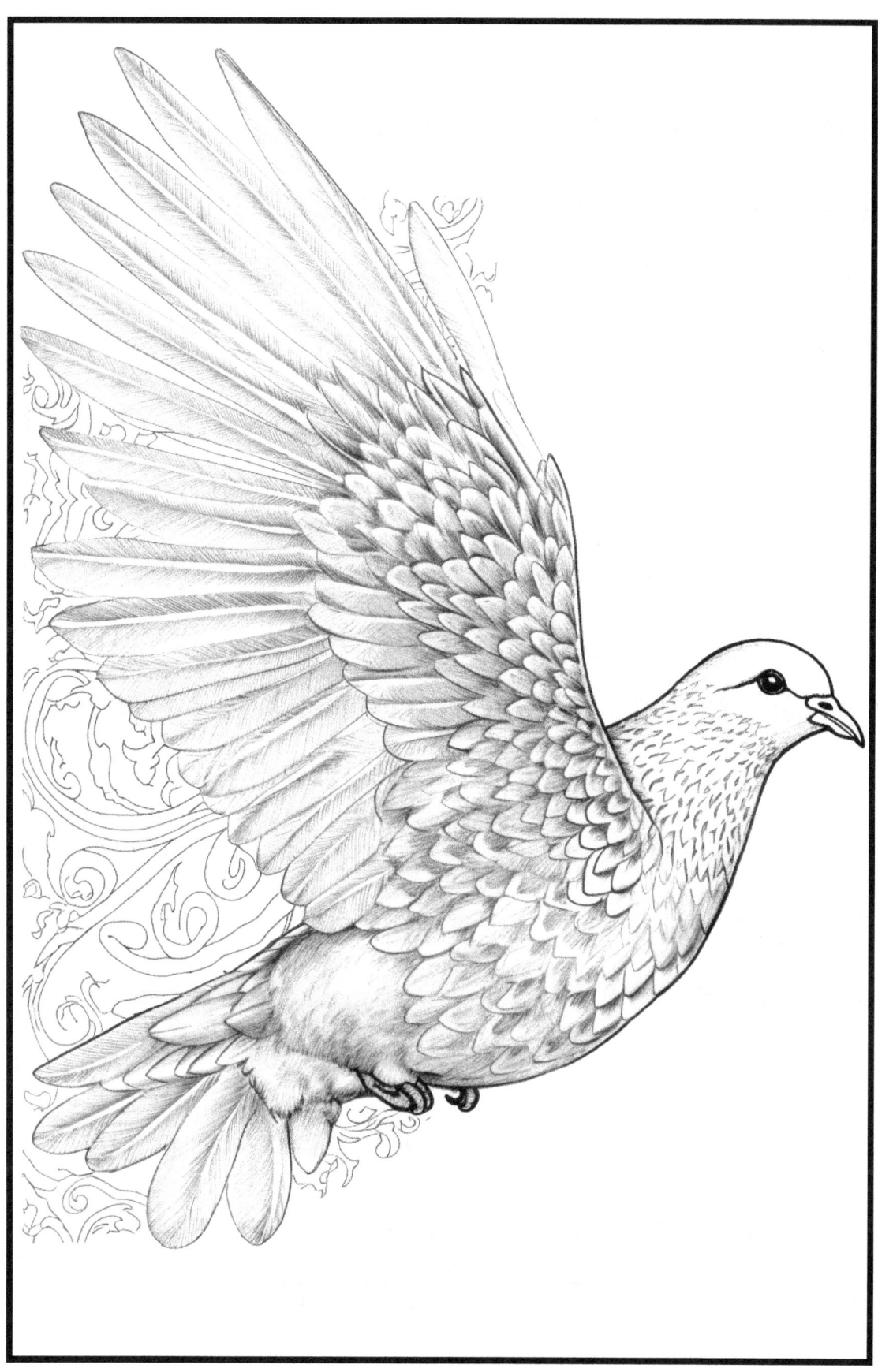

The book of 2 John is a brief letter written by the apostle John, emphasizing the importance of truth, love, and obedience within the Christian community. It warns against welcoming false teachers and urges believers to remain faithful to the teachings of Jesus Christ. The central quote from 2 John 1:6 encapsulates this message: "And this is love: that we walk in obedience to his commands. As you have heard from the beginning, his command is that you walk in love." This verse highlights the inseparable connection between love and obedience, emphasizing the need for Christians to live out their faith with sincerity and fidelity. A path diverging into two, symbolizing the choice between truth and falsehood.

2 JOHN

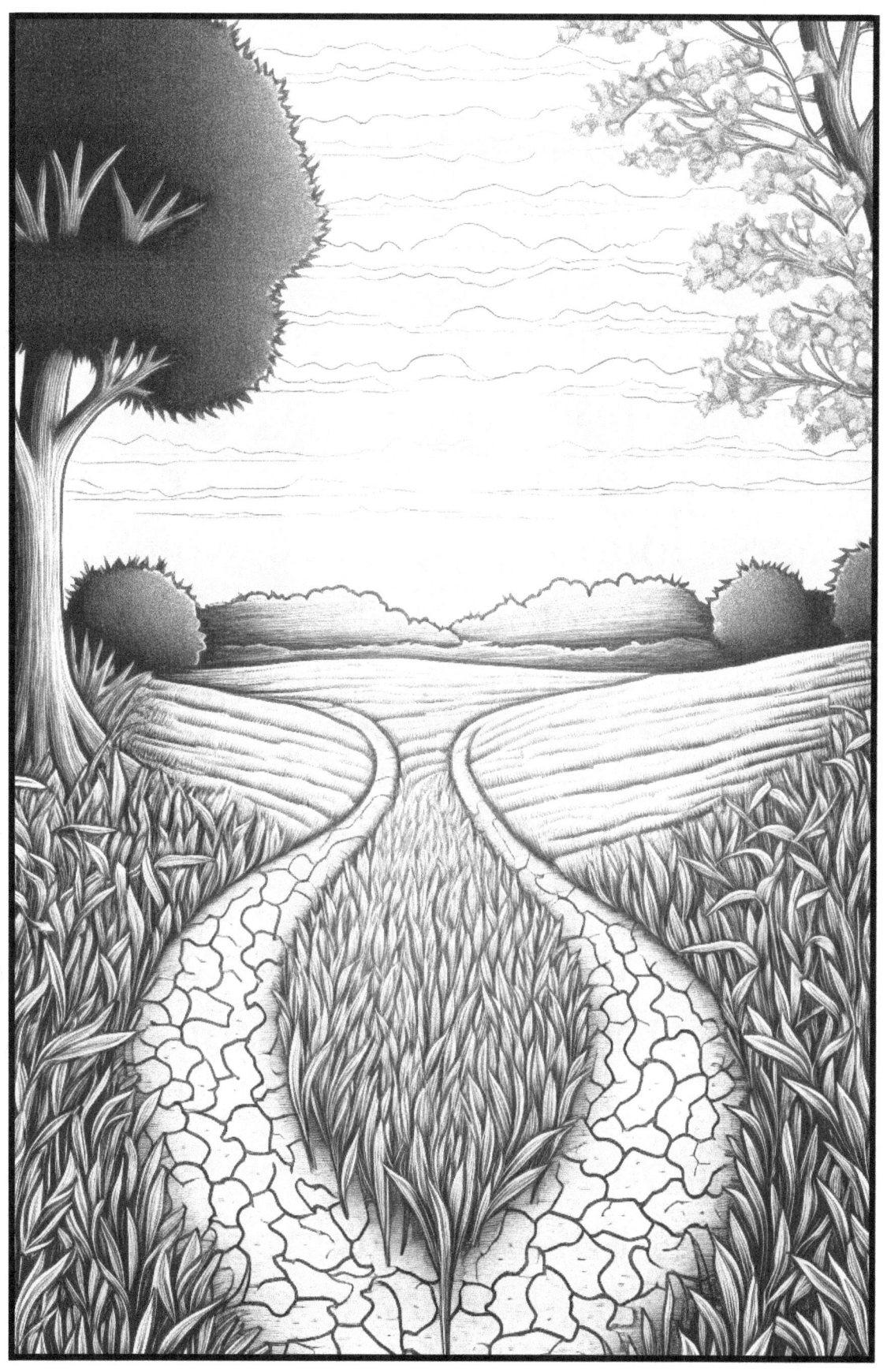

The book of 3 John is a short letter written by the apostle John to Gaius, commending him for his hospitality and urging him to continue supporting fellow believers. It emphasizes the importance of hospitality and cooperation in spreading the truth and supporting those who are engaged in God's work. A key verse that captures this message is found in 3 John 1:8, which states, "We ought therefore to show hospitality to such people so that we may work together for the truth." This verse encourages believers to extend hospitality to those who are faithfully serving God, recognizing that by doing so, they participate in advancing the truth of the Gospel. Illustrating the idea of cooperation and collaboration in supporting one another in God's work. This can represent the mutual effort to advance the truth of the Gospel..

3 JOHN

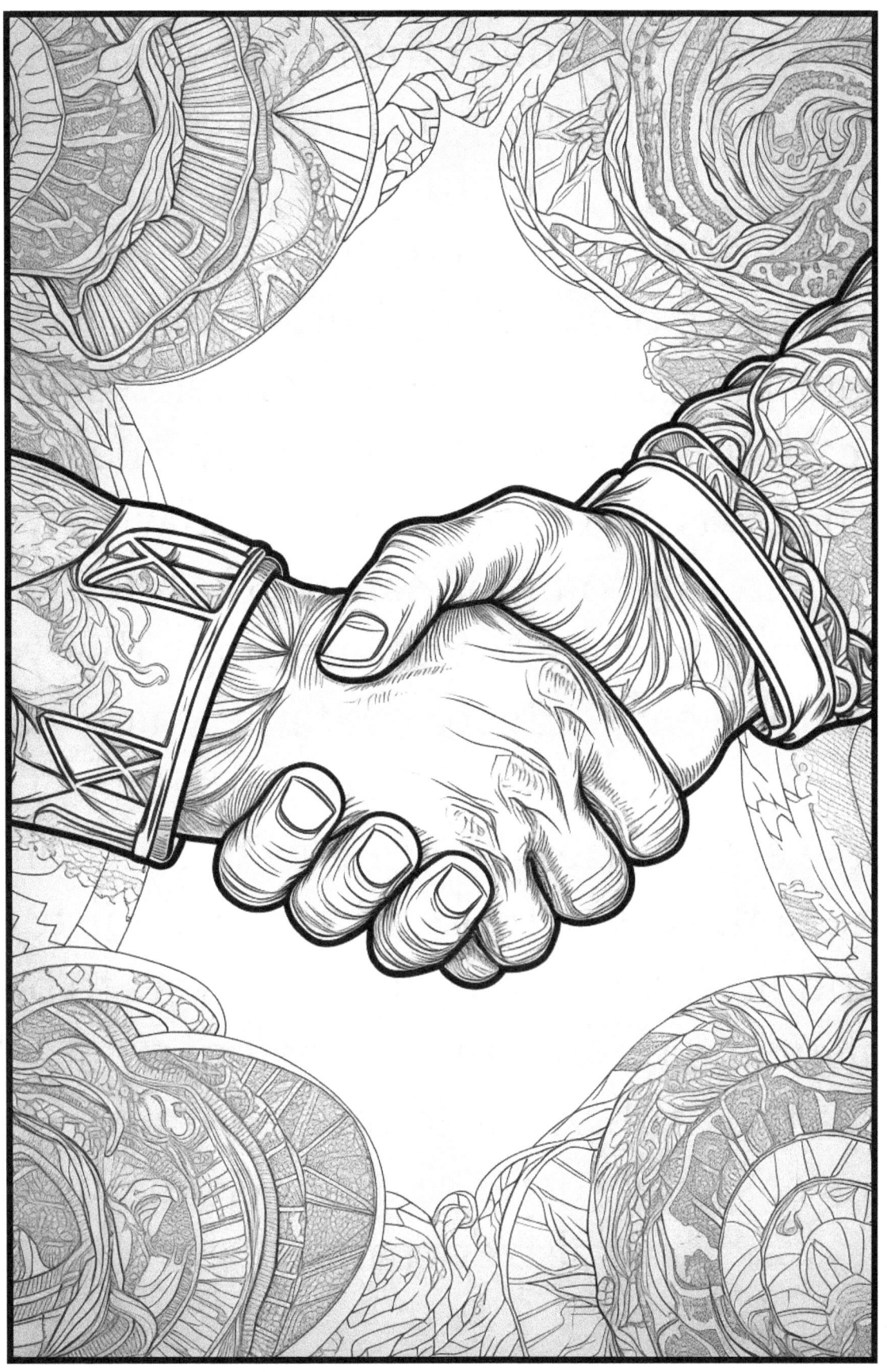

The book of Jude in the New Testament serves as a warning against false teachers and emphasizes the need for believers to contend earnestly for the faith. It highlights the importance of standing firm in the truth and guarding against deceptive influences. Jude 1:3 captures this sentiment, saying, "Beloved, while I was making every effort to write you about our common salvation, I felt the necessity to write to you appealing that you contend earnestly for the faith which was once for all handed down to the saints." This verse emphasizes the urgency of defending the faith against those who seek to distort and undermine it, calling believers to be vigilant and unwavering in their commitment to the truth. A shield representing the believer's active defense of the Gospel against false doctrines.

JUDE

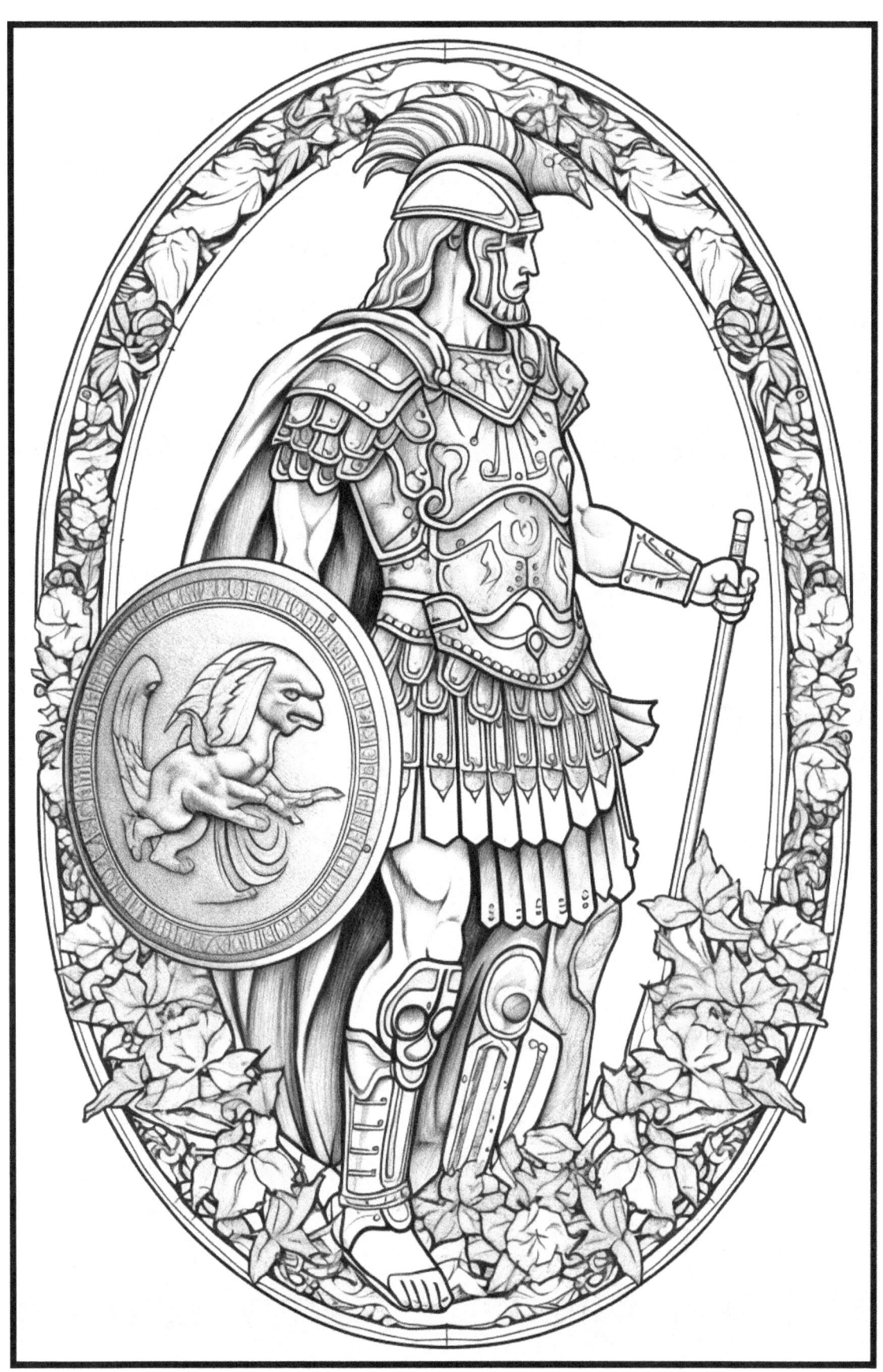

The book of Revelation, the final book in the New Testament, is a complex and highly symbolic work that unveils apocalyptic visions and prophetic messages. It provides a glimpse into the ultimate triumph of God's sovereignty and the consummation of His redemptive plan. Revelation 21:5 beautifully captures the promise of a new creation: "And he who was seated on the throne said, 'Behold, I am making all things new.'" This verse speaks of the transformative power of God, who brings forth a new heaven and a new earth, where righteousness and eternal glory reign. The book of Revelation is filled with vivid imagery, cosmic battles, heavenly worship, and the ultimate victory of Jesus Christ, depicting the culmination of God's divine plan for humanity and the restoration of all things. The Tree of Life and the River of Life: Symbols of eternal blessings and the restoration of all things, signifying the new heaven and new earth.

REVELATION

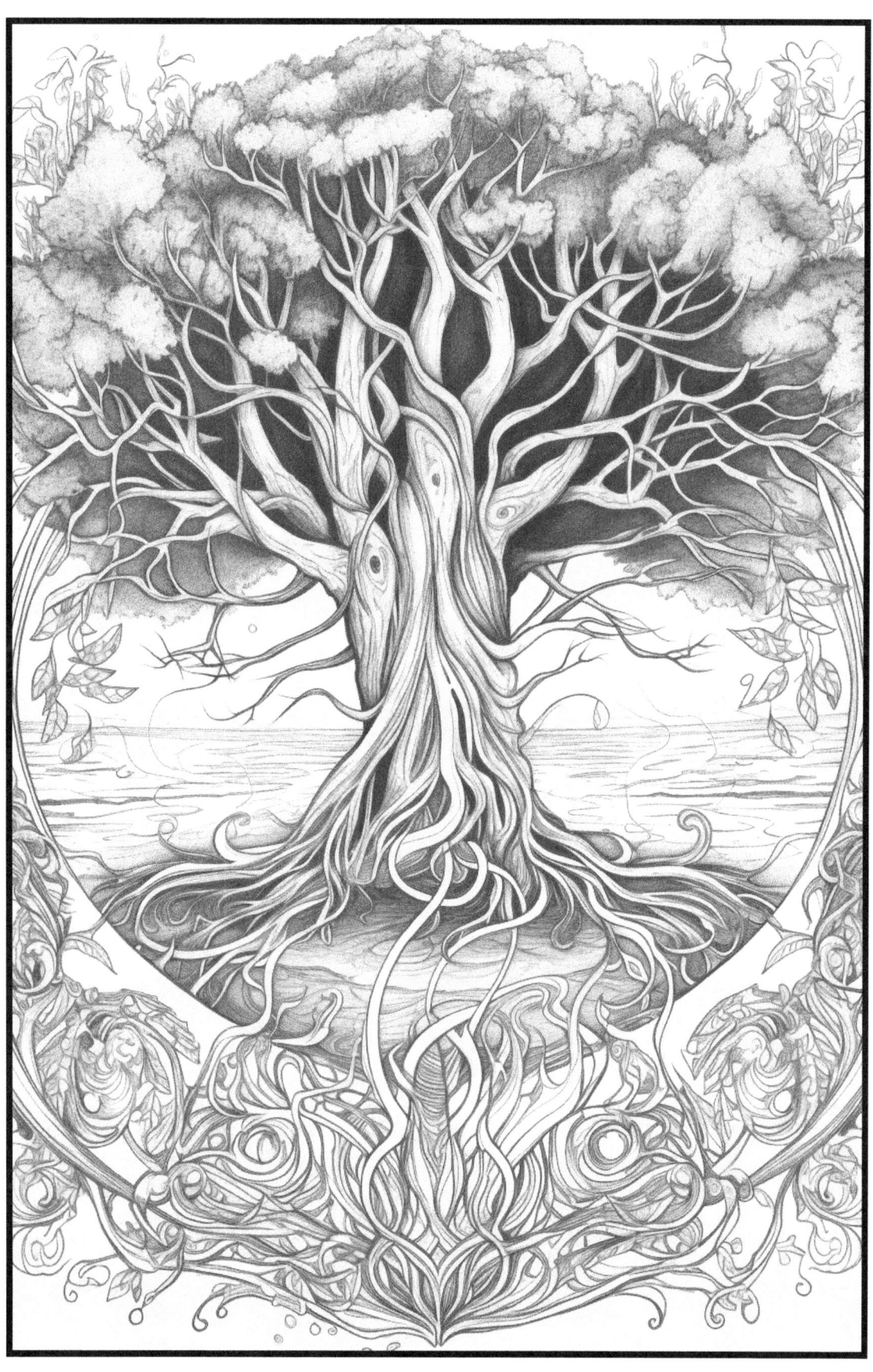